THE NEGRO IN
FEDERAL EMPLOYMENT

THE NEGRO IN FEDERAL EMPLOYMENT

The Quest for Equal Opportunity

Samuel Krislov

Classics of the Social Sciences

Quid Pro Books
New Orleans, Louisiana

The Negro in Federal Employment

Copyright © 2012 by Samuel Krislov. All rights reserved. No part of this book may be reproduced in any form or by any means without permission in writing from the current publisher.

Originally published in 1967 by the University of Minnesota Press, Minneapolis, Minnesota, and copyright © 1967 by the University of Minnesota. This is an unabridged and authorized edition.

Published in 2012 by Quid Pro Books.

ISBN 978-1-61027-153-0 (pbk)
ISBN 978-1-61027-154-7 (eBook)

Quid Pro, LLC
5860 Citrus Blvd., Suite D-101
New Orleans, Louisiana 70123
www.quidprobooks.com

qp

Publisher's Cataloging-in-Publication

Krislov, Samuel.

  The Negro in Federal Employment: The Quest for Equal Opportunity / Samuel Krislov.

  p. cm. — (Classics of the social sciences)

  Includes index and biographical note references; includes 2012 foreword and preface.

1. African Americans—employment. 2. Civil service—United States. 3. Representative government and representation—United States. I. Krislov, Samuel. II. Title. III. Series.

JK723.N4 K7 2012   321.43'.733—dc22
                                                                        2012287492

The material in this book is drawn in part from the author's essay, "Government and Equal Employment Opportunity" published in *Employment, Race, and Poverty*, edited by Arthur M. Ross and Herbert Hill, copyright © 1967 by Harcourt, Brace & World, Inc.

Printed in the United States of America.

*To my children
and their children
with hopes for a more nearly fair world.*

TABLE OF CONTENTS

Page numbers in brackets below reference the original pagination (these numbers are embedded into text in this edition by the use of brackets). Page numbers shown to the right below (and without brackets) refer to the current pagination of this edition, found at bottoms of the pages.

Foreword [2012] i

Preface [2012] v

Acknowledgments [1967] ix

INTRODUCTION...{3} 1

1 • THE NEGRO AND THE FEDERAL GOVERNMENT
    BEFORE WORLD WAR II...{7} 5

2 • THE NEGRO AND THE FEDERAL SERVICE IN AN ERA
    OF CHANGE...{28} 23

3 • REPRESENTATIVE BUREAUCRACY AND CIVIL RIGHTS...{46} 39

4 • MERIT, CIVIL RIGHTS, AND CIVIL SERVICE...{65} 55

5 • NEGRO EMPLOYMENT, AN ANALYSIS...{86} 73

6 • THE MACHINERY OF EQUALITY...{106} 91

7 • THE PROBLEM IN THE DEPARTMENTS: SOME
    ILLUSTRATIONS ...{123} 105

CONCLUSIONS...{143} 123

INDEX...{151} 131

About the Author 137

Foreword

I read *The Negro in Federal Employment* for the first time within a year or so of its 1967 publication. I was interested in two topics on which the book seemed likely to throw light. One was the particular aspect of the struggle for civil rights (then in what seemed like full flood) that the book sought to examine, namely the participation of Negroes in the Federal service. I came to my initial reading without really having previously considered that participation—at least not systematically, and not as an important front in the civil rights struggle; and so the book was informational, and provided the light I had anticipated. The second topic that interested me was the author, Samuel Krislov, whom I was getting to know as a mentor during my graduate school years at the University of Minnesota. The book helped to persuade me that Sam was a distinctive writer and an insightful analyst, who often identified issues and perspectives that I might not have seen or considered without his having pointed them out. Both are qualities one would want in a mentor. Figuring that out was enlightening.

Recently, then, tasked with penning a fresh introduction, I have re-read the book—more than four decades since first opening it. It seems natural to ask what significance(s) it may have now. I think there are at least three categories to consider.

The first is well-expressed as a question: *what has endured*? What parts of a 1967 analysis can be commended to a 21st-century reader? I would start with the first two chapters. Concisely, in just a few pages, the reader of this slim volume is offered a very useful history (or pair of histories) of *The Negro and the Federal Government Before World War II* and *The Negro and the Federal Service in an Era of Change*. Nicely summarizing a substantial body of scholarship, the former (Chapter 1) touches lightly on the severely limited opportunities for service by blacks at the nation's founding, and continues deftly to sketch political traditions that dominated conditions to the eve of World War II. Krislov summarizes thusly, at page 19 of the 1967 printing:

> ... political patronage had proved an inadequate means to expanded Negro opportunity. It was rather the civil service, with its merit system, that opened the way to Negro participation in public life.

i

The latter (Chapter 2) again concisely summarizes not only a substantial scholarship, but also draws essential information from government reports and print media. The concluding Section IV of the chapter suitably offers a slightly more detailed view of actions taken/not taken by the Johnson administration, then as now considered a strong source of initiatives in the struggle for civil rights.

> So a first answer is: read the book for the historical scholarship, and expect to grasp major themes in an economical rendering.

A second kind of continuing usefulness is in the realm of intellectual history. At least two enduring strands of conceptual work were very usefully forwarded, if not quite invented, here: *representative bureaucracy* in Chapter 3, and *merit*, as pursued in Chapter 4. As to the former, Section IV in Chapter 3 sets the stage for subsequent analyses of representative bureaucracy (including Krislov's own) by outlining rationales for representative bureaucracies, and conceptually pointing toward ways of measuring the representativeness of bureaucracies. As to merit, the conceptual work is eventually tied, usefully, to the claims of blacks for places in the federal service. Yet the conceptual work, especially in Section II of Chapter 4, stands nicely by itself, and is a useful primer for many debates that we have seen in the period following 1967 (and that are surely still to come). What can it mean to demand compensation for American Indians displaced more than a century ago—or for Nisei who were herded into internment camps circa 1942? How should we understand the import of California's Proposition 209 (adopted in 1996, prohibiting the consideration of race, sex, or ethnicity in public employment, public education, and public contracting)? Much of course has been written on those questions—my point is that in a few words, Krislov offers a still-useful primer. And in doing so, the analysis in this volume appears to anticipate the battles over affirmative action, and more broadly over who gets what, when, and how in contests featuring groups identified by race or national origin.[1]

> So a second answer is: read the book for the primers on topics of continuing interest, especially representative bureau-

---

[1] Compare, e.g., Edward Flores, Jillian Medeiros, & Harry P. Pachon, *Equal Employment Opportunity or Enclave Employment?: A Critique of the GAO Report on Hispanic Employment in Federal Agencies*, The Tomás Rivera Policy Institute (Jan. 2007). The analytic reference is to The Equal Employment Opportunity Commission, *Annual Report on the Federal Work Force Fiscal Year 2007* (last modified on Aug. 19, 2008) (FY 2007 Annual Report), *available at* http://www.eeoc.gov/federal/fsp2007/index.html.

Foreword

cracy and the merit/equality debates endemic to the operation of civil service systems.

The idea of what may have been anticipated in this book takes me to a third kind of continuing usefulness. Let me again phrase it as a question: *what can we appreciate by looking back* on a work that, in part, sought to peer into a then-unknown future from the vantage of 1967? Part of this appreciation is holistic. My re-reading led me to recall a mid-1960s sense of hopefulness about improving the general condition of African-Americans in the United States, and the sense of moral commitment to civil rights.

More specifically, in the matter of forecasting the development of policy, the view from 1967 was reasonably far-sighted. For example, Krislov displays a pretty good sense of the possibility of extension of EEOC rights enforcement to groups in addition to African-Americans. Explicitly mentioned in the concluding chapter are "other minorities like women and the handicapped." And the rhetorical gesture seems to me to foreshadow efforts to prohibit discrimination based on age or pregnancy status, perhaps even discrimination based on sexual orientation. Not much discussed here—out of scope for a book on federal employment—are the now-familiar extensions of EEOC-style enforcement of anti-discrimination public policies to state and local governments. But it's easy to see that the forecast in 1967 was accurately for increases in African-American federal, and by extension in public, employment. As recently noted by the University of California's Center for Labor Research and Education, more than 21% of black workers had public sector jobs in the 2008-2010 period, compared with a little more than 16% of non-black workers. Calculated slightly differently, blacks were 30 percent more likely than non-blacks to work in the public sector in the noted years.[2]

> So a third answer is: read the book to recapture the sense of the times when the civil rights movement was near the top of the national agenda, and seemed unambiguously the right course of action. Yet read the book also to derive a sense of how a strong political science analysis can anticipate future policy developments—in general, of course, but with a nice eye for probable evolution and extension of governmental commitment.

In all, this is a slim yet significant book, open to a fresh appreciation. Look over the concise histories. Don't miss the conceptual work on repre-

---

[2] Steven Pitts (April, 2011), Research Brief: Black Workers and the Public Sector. Retrieved July 25, 2012, from http://laborcenter.berkeley.edu/blackworkers/blacks_public_sector11.pdf.

sentative bureaucracies, merit and equality. Noticing the anticipation of policy growth and development, give thought to work by political scientists who may be similarly forecasting policy futures.

And give thought also to duly appreciating the enduring worth of scholarship by insightful analysts, such as Sam Krislov.

KEITH BOYUM
*Professor Emeritus of Political Science,
California State University, Fullerton*

Fullerton, California
August 2012

Preface

In the period that I taught in the Political Science Department at Michigan State University, it was widely known as a place of intellectual stimulation set in a tumultuous atmosphere, a Hobbesian state of nature. A colleague told me his Ph.D. advisor's last admonition to him as he set off for East Lansing was "I usually tell my fledgling Ph.D.s 'don't buy a house until you get tenure.' Since you are going to Michigan State, I advise you not to buy any heavy furniture."

Things could move rapidly in your favor as well. I had had several discussions with Herb Garfinkel about my hopes to take advantage of the government's annual compilation of equal employment data, a compliance study with the bonus of the government collecting the data. But my plate was full. I had contracts to do two books and a case study of what happens when an attorney general feels litigation he is supposed to defend is unconstitutional.

Herb came in one day to inform me he had rejected a research appointment in the MSU School of Labor and Industrial Relations, but had suggested my name and project to them. Einar Hardin, the Institute's Director, clearly was very interested and he contacted me for an outline the next day. Within a week I was appointed an associate in the School and had one quarter of research each year to get started and to move my other projects along as well. Herb also recommended me to Herbert Hill and Arthur Ross, who were compiling a volume on race and employment. While that meant I had to write quickly, it also got the project off to a quick start.

Einar had indicated that grants of any size would help him in budgetary infighting. As a result I applied for several small grants and given the hot button topic of my project, I got them all. I was also able to arrange visiting scholar privileges at Brookings giving me a phone drop for Washington appointments. As an added bonus I shared an office with Ted Lowi, then on exile from Cornell, which afforded memorable conversations.

It worked out beautifully. I would plan a trip, usually starting Sunday evening by taking the Grand Trunk Railway, a Canadian owned spur that ran from Lansing to Chicago. There I took a Pennsylvania railroad train with a coach ticket. I would contact the conductor about a step-up rate for a tiny Pullman cubicle which I invariably got. I had purchased dictaphone equipment since the secretaries preferred oral dictation over deciphering my handwriting. I transcribed routine manuscripts for an hour or two. Arriving early in the morning in Washington, I would have breakfast at Scholl's cafeteria and check in either at the wonderful Sheraton Carleton or the Washington Hilton across the street. Both chains had a $10 a night faculty rate and I would have reserved in advance. I would then check my messages at Brookings, and if there were open times, would proceed to try to get other interviews. In stray moments I could use the facilities of the Library of Congress to fill in gaps in the very uneven Michigan State collections.

I found I enjoyed interviewing very much. I did not use a set schedule of questions, relying on the fact that I had published data to work with. I bore in mind a half dozen or so set questions which I interspersed when discussions lagged. It was harder to schedule interviews than to extract information or to sustain discussion. Often the appointment was scheduled with limits on the time, but interviewees once talking not only did not usually invoke those limits, they even went on when I concluded I got all the information I could and tried to cut the appointment short. Two decades later, I used the same techniques in Europe when I worked on a European Community study but my collaborator Claus Ehlermann was the Director of Legal Services for the Community sitting in on all Commission meetings and used the Community liaison offices to open doors for me. On the other hand, my brother, a social security researcher at the University of Kentucky, found interviewing abroad more difficult than in the U.S. When he suggested to a Swedish pension officer that the lack of a bulletin board listing offices occupied by officials made public access difficult, he was crisply told: "In Europe we do not work for the public, but for the government." In my years of interviewing, American bureaucrats felt they were working for the public.

A conclusion that has remained in my memory was of the immense variety of skills and talent possessed by bureaucrats bearing the same label and rank. Some agencies used the equal employment officer to solve a personnel problem such as alcoholism especially when they didn't value the program and its intent. I was not surprised to be told years later that some police departments dumped problem employees in similar fashion into their science detection units where they confounded innocence and guilt but did not interfere with normal routines. At the other extreme the head of the Patent Office assigned himself the task since he thought bridging a caste system was the agency's main problem. The office was divided between white professionals and black menials who mainly retrieved printed documents on patents from dusty bins often rodent- or insect-infested. His task of integration was complicated by the ongoing replacement of the primitive system of printing and storage of patents by the new technology of printing on demand only.

I have two regrets. I always thought that my approach to merit as a set of nesting concepts from different vantage points has not been given adequate attention. That chapter was reprinted in a book on professionalism, but I think was more creative than that. Like any father I feel protective of my neglected ideas as well as any overlooked virtues of my children. For a brief

Preface

ten weeks I shared an office with Herman Finer, then recently retired from the University of Chicago. He in return shared with me his erudition and wisdom. Over the years he had concluded that we were uniquely poor judges of different aspects of our work. I sometimes accept that view; most of the time I feel the idea was underappreciated.

More personally and clearly my own fault, I regret being unable to make use of what had attracted me to the project in the first place—the compilation of vast amounts of data over time. I had hoped to be able to compare organizations with other bureaucratic structures, but ended lamely using only year-to-year comparisons of the same ones. I console myself with the fact that equal opportunity officers and other scholars including statisticians haven't been able to use the material either. The shifts in composition within a single agency were often informative and useful when compared to previous years, but even then were shaped by other factors including the skills of bureaucrats in producing paper results sought by their masters. Among the problems that complicated the data were the massive differences in size of the units. The bulk of federal employees are in a handful of operations, while myriad pygmy operations really would be excluded by a careful statistician as outliers.

After all, equal opportunity was a sideshow in the operation of government and policy—and even a minor part of the quest for efficiency and the need for rules and regulations. Such normal conditions as veterans' privilege and the right of displaced bureaucrats to claim vacant positions in other units, and similar operations of rules relating to employment, could and did overwhelm affirmative action most of the time.

No doubt, the annual reports and the constant attention of "improvement" demanded by John Macy, who headed all aspects of employment under President Lyndon Johnson, reflected the President's determination that equal opportunity not be ignored in the flow of events. There is also little doubt that administrators got the message, but the statistics that were produced were more a symbol than a reality.

I also have two positive feelings about my achievement and peer acceptance. The chapters on the history of blacks in the federal service were written with the conviction that the link with the past is not a duty, only a necessity. It was lucky that Paul Van Riper's still definitive history of the civil service was published while I was working on my project. I also drew heavily on fine dissertations by Laurence Hayes and William Bradbury. It is gratifying that Frank Thompson has included a condensation of my chapters in his *Classics of Public Personnel Administration.*

If anything, by comparison, my work on representative bureaucracy has been over-recognized. I reoriented the concept away from the originator J. Donald Kingsley's weak insight that bureaucrats are middle-class mandarins and scribes. I called attention to the fact that the real concerns of modern times revolve around gender, ethnicity and race ,and degrees of diversity. With that I helped call attention to the centrality of representative bureaucracy in worldwide intersocietal conflicts. Ingenious researchers have particularized and developed tests to determine whether the claims of its importance are merited. Theorists and empiricists like Frederick Mosher, Kenneth Maier, and David Rosenbloom have added nuances, depth, and precision to the concept. I am proud to be in their company.

A note about the name of this book: The original project was entitled "Civil Rights and Civil Service" and my original paperwork with the University of Minnesota Press actually refers to it by this title. The editor, who was a friend of a friend, strongly urged me to use the word "Negro" in the title as it would boost sales—it would sound more contemporary. About a year later, the term became taboo and sales nosedived. It certainly no longer sounds contemporary. My current publisher strongly urged me to retain the title from the original edition as a gesture toward authenticity, and because this is the name under which the study has been known and referenced for 45 years. I am once again pliable.

SAMUEL KRISLOV

Professor Emeritus of
Political Science and Law,
University of Minnesota

Bethesda, Maryland
August 2012

Acknowledgments

{*page* vii *in original*}

Even a slender volume generates many obligations. This study began while I was a research associate of the School of Labor and Industrial Relations of Michigan State University, and I am indebted to the directors and associates of the School, especially Einar Hardin, for helping one clarify my own quest. Support for continuation of the study has been made available by the Graduate School of the University of Minnesota, and small but strategically timed grants were made to this and to a closely related project by the Society for the Psychological Study of Social Issues, the National Institute of Mental Health, the American Philosophical Society, and the Louis Rabinowitz Fund. The Brookings Institution was kind enough to designate me visiting scholar and thus provided a research office for an itinerant investigator. Portions of this study—principally Chapter 5—draw upon an earlier essay written for the University of California Industrial Relations Center and published in a symposium edited by Arthur Ross and Herbert Hill. To them, and to the other participants in that venture, I am indebted for cogent criticism. Myrna Smith acted as typist and research assistant, and Malcolm Feeley, Homer Williamson, Sharon Rogers, and others in my seminar on the executive process contributed to my own education. Professors Harold Chase and David Fellman read the manuscript critically and {viii} constructively, and Jeanne Sinnen of the University of Minnesota Press assisted far more than an author has a right to expect. Needless to say, neither the individuals nor the institutions mentioned are fairly culpable for any of the remaining shortcomings, or for the opinions expressed, in the following pages.

— S. K.
March 1967

THE NEGRO IN
FEDERAL EMPLOYMENT

Introduction

{page 3 in original}
FOR over a decade our nation—our civilization—has been consciously engaged in a quest for social justice far-reaching enough to satisfy the most visionary dreamers of the American dream. That task has proven to be a conglomerate one; the effort to end legal and spatial segregation of our nonwhite citizens has in turn engendered a drive toward their dispersion by social class and occupation, toward an end to poverty-by-skin-color. Such an effort is not unique in human history—the example of India and its untouchables comes readily to mind; yet it may fairly be said that history records many more attempts, and gives more explicit guidance in techniques, to subjugate minorities than to socially elevate them.

What seems unprecedented is the combination of scope of social change sought and speed with which it is desired. This is related to the unprecedented amount of attention focused on our effort, the unrelenting concern of other peoples with our success or failure. Equal opportunity has become a litmus test for our entire society. Our progress toward it is being watched as a crucial indicator of the possibility of harmonious interrelations among different races—a possibility of immense though increasingly less hopeful significance for societies of Africa and Asia, and of vital importance for the international relations {4} of the future. Our effort to achieve equal opportunity is regarded—quite properly so—as proof of our genuine collective attitude toward racial equality. In a deeper sense, too, our accomplishments in this area are an earnest of our belief in and commitment to the American value system, so fervently and on the whole consistently articulated throughout the world. The recent change in race relations reflects our consciousness of world attention, but more than that it also reflects our own willingness to live up to the best standards of that system, to eradicate the inconsistency which Myrdal so aptly labeled "the American dilemma." No doubt the pressures of world opinion and the new geographic concentration of Negro population, with concomitant increase in political power, have played a role in "searing the consciences" of white Americans which like all consciences tend to be most sensitive when sensitized. In the end, however, "conscience" looms as the key word; as Harry Kalven put it in his brilliant study, *The Negro and the First Amendment*, the civil rights movement has been a successful "attempt to entrap democracy in its own decencies."

Much has been learned in the course of that attempt. The superficial view of the South as sole culprit has been replaced by a sense of the national dimensions of the racial problem. It has become clear that the North's record of devotion to equality is less than pristine, as witnessed most recently in its counter-demonstrations and violent reaction to peaceful petitioners. Historical evidence suggests, too, that social ingenuity on behalf of discrimination has not been a regional phenomenon, Rather, by a social "Gresham's Law," novel prejudiced practice has been initiated in each part of the country and imitated elsewhere. Thus school segregation was a northern pre-Civil War custom, and residential segregation was for a long period more pronounced and stricter in the North than in the South. That prejudice comes easy, and is not confined to any specific geographic locale, is evidenced by the recent turn of British public opinion from smug and even supercilious condemnation of racism to smug and vicious condonation when immigrants from Britain's West Indies possessions presented the British for the first time with a problem of social integration of Negroes.

Other simplifications have been abandoned. Analyses that found one factor as cause and cure—the vote or lack thereof, economic position, even so complex a matter as family structure—seem naïve, in the light of reality. Inequality is an institutionalized aspect of American life, with {5} legal, psychological, economic, and social buttresses. Our unfortunate heritage is clearly revealed in many ways, even in the derivation of certain words like "niggardly" and "denigrate." It has been recognized that such institutionalized prejudice of diverse origins can be overcome only by institutionalized change that alters diverse patterns.

Recognition of this fact has indeed proceeded to the point where there is a need to reassert priorities and define strategies. Today, the civil rights effort seems much like the action of Stephen Leacock's hero, who "flung himself from the room, flung himself upon his horse and rode madly off in all directions." When legal barriers were major obstacles, of necessity and symbolically they were primary targets. No such obvious strategy is apparent today. There seems to be a need for objective analysis of limited segments of the civil rights movement in order to identify some of the paths that may profitably be followed in the future.

The present study deals with one facet of the quest for equality the equal employment program in the federal service. It is an attempt to describe and to evaluate the major elements of that program, to put the issues in historical and administrative context, to provide some of the long-range perspective absent in discussions of societal needs by those directly and emotionally involved with day-to-day issues. A social movement of the magnitude of that in which our society is engaged requires participants in various roles. But this book is a product of my conviction that much of today's fashionable emphasis upon empathy and total absorption is not only misplaced but even deleterious.

Several factors seem to justify the extensive treatment here of this particular program. One of these factors is the long-term growth of the public sector as a source of employment. This growth in recent years, however, has occurred largely at the state and local levels, areas touched on only lightly here. More significant is the "multiplier" importance of public service—great changes in a wide arena are instigated by small alterations in governmental

Introduction

personnel policy. The symbolic role of public position should not be overlooked. In seeking to implement the goal of greater equality in society generally government has a special responsibility to come to others with clean hands. If the elimination of prejudice cannot be achieved in the public bureaucracy it is unlikely that it will be achieved anywhere.

This study is based upon interviews conducted during the period {6} 1963-1965 in every department and virtually every agency—supervised by the President's Committee on Equal Employment Opportunity. It necessarily, then, deals with operation of the equal employment program before assumption of responsibility for the program by the Civil Service Commission in 1966. Although the rules and machinery established by the commission are discussed, no attempt is made to evaluate their impact. Indeed, given the size of the bureaucracy, the pace of complaints, and the subtlety of bureaucratic change, it would probably be unwise and unfair to do so for two or three years. The emphasis in the study is, in any event, upon institutional and programmatic aspects, rather than upon internal politics or personalities.

For the convenience of the reader, a word seems desirable about the structure of this book. It essentially can be divided into three main topics. The opening two chapters constitute a historical sketch of the Negro in the federal service. Chapters 3 and 4 deal with two concepts central to evaluation of success or failure of the equal employment program—representative bureaucracy and merit. Consideration of these seems essential in any discussion of equality in public employment, for they are the perimeters within which demands may be made for office—and in the light of which public acquiescence or denial can be judged. Finally, the remaining chapters provide a description of the equal employment program and its achievements. Some of my colleagues who were kind enough to read the manuscript have suggested—with some logic—that Chapters 3 and 4, which deal with more contemporary implications, might well precede the historical discussion. I have retained the order that seemed to me most natural, but a reader who prefers the former approach may choose to begin with Chapter 3.

1

The Negro and the Federal Government
Before World War II

I

{7}
THE mode of arrival of the Negro on American shores was hardly calculated to enhance his future claims to public office. Brought to this country under conditions of extreme and protracted horror of a type only recently fully delineated by historians and compared by Stanley Elkins to concentration camp conditions the Negro found himself at the bottom, even in a society predominantly graded into various conditions of servitude.[1] The fact of skin color made his servitude more certain and escape less possible. His cultural and political backwardness left him vulnerable to violation and continuous diminution of his limited legal rights. Other groups advanced in colonial society; the Negroes lost such status as, they initially had. From servitude they slipped into slavery. English common law knew no such institution; the honor of rediscovering its barbarism belongs to the "free new world."

The intimate connection between the Negro race and the institution {8} of slavery remains the key to the Negro's low estate. Since virtually all. Americans of African blood are the descendants of slaves, the connotations of slavery are inevitably the heritage of each individual Negro. As Tocqueville so eloquently put it, "The tradition of slavery dishonors the race, and the peculiarity of the race perpetuates the tradition of slavery." The problem is passed on even under conditions of freedom. "To induce the whites to abandon the opinion they have conceived of the moral and intellectual inferiority of their former slaves, the Negroes must change; but as long as this opinion persists,

---

[1] Stanley Elkins, *Slavery* (Chicago: University of Chicago Press, 1959). Elkins, develops the thesis that the "total" slavery situation, in which there was no concession of any of the rights of humanity such as a stable family relationship, had profound characterological effects upon Negro personality and Negro institutions. See also Frank Tannenbaum's seminal *Slave and Citizen* (New York: Knopf, 1947). A clue to the emergence of this totalitarian slavery is perhaps to be found in Alfred Conrad and John Meyer's conclusion that plantation slavery required breeding to make it economically profitable. See their *The Economics of Slavery* (Chicago: Aldine, 1964), especially p. 82.

they cannot change."² This is the Negro dilemma, stated a century before the conflict between the values of equality and race prejudice was discovered as the white dilemma.

Obviously, the Negro slave could not become an officeholder, whether elective or appointive. The freed man found his prospects hardly greater. Rejection of slavery, Tocqueville noted, did not make the white residents of a state more friendly to the Negro; rather, it was more usual to find overt hostility. The state of Ohio, for example, forbade both slavery and the residence of free Negroes. In Illinois, Indiana, and Oregon, prohibition of Negro immigration was in the state constitution, In the state of New York the radical Democratic followers of Andrew Jackson and Martin Van Buren were the successful agitators for a policy of restricting suffrage to only a small minority of the free Negro population of that state, Anti-Negro slogans and other indications of race prejudice were common in New York political campaigns of the 1830's.

From the establishment of the nation it was on the whole taken for granted that federal service was limited to whites, Even during the Revolutionary War, George Washington had been extremely reluctant to utilize Negro troops in spite of the shortage of men. Negroes were on July 10, 1775, refused permission to re-enlist or to enlist from that date forward as new troops, Only under the duress of absolute necessity, including a declaration by Lord Dunmore, Virginia's royal governor, offering freedom to Negro slaves joining the British, did Washington later reverse himself and accept the use of free Negroes as agents of independence. Thus at the nadir of slaveholding influence, at a time when the cotton gin had not made slavery profitable, when the Declaration {9} of Independence had come within a hairsbreadth of calling for the end of the slave trade, public service was for all practical purposes not open to even those Negroes who had been formally and legally freed. Nor was this ever a trivial number; the 1860 census, for example, showed that 12 percent of all Negroes were free.³

In the small and fumbling bureaucracy that was established under the Articles of Confederation and the only slightly more efficient one that took form under the Constitution, there seems to have been a pervasive assumption that no appointments of Negroes would be made, except as messengers and laborers, and even these in minuscule numbers.⁴ But in only one area relating to employment was there explicit statutory reference to Negroes. Ironically, the postal service today perhaps the most prominent utilizer of

---

[2] Alexis De Tocqueville, *Democracy in America* (New York: Vintage, 1954), Vol. I, pp. 372 and n. 32.

[3] Arnold Rose, *Assuring Freedom to the Free* (Detroit: Wayne State University Press, 1965), p. 35. See also Richard Wade, *Slavery in the Cities* (New York: Oxford University Press, 1964).

[4] *Crisis*, November 1928, p. 389.

Negro manpower of all federal agencies was expressly closed to nonwhite employment. Color was mentioned in a few other early acts of Congress: in 1790 Congress limited naturalization to white aliens and in 1792 limited enrollment in the militia to white males; in 1820 it authorized citizens of Washington to elect white city officials. However, administrative rulings carried discrimination further, extending even to refusal to grant Negroes passports.[5]

The Post Office provision had in many ways the most interesting history. In 1802 in a confidential letter to the chairman of a Senate committee, Postmaster General Gideon Granger urged its passage, suggesting there were objections to Negro mail carriers "of a nature too delicate to engraft into a report which may become public, yet too important to be omitted or passed over without full consideration." Such a role as distributing the mail might teach Negroes the pernicious doctrine "that a man's rights do not depend on his color." The Postmaster General cautioned against "everything which tends to increase their knowledge of natural rights, of men and things, or that affords them an opportunity of associating, acquiring and commuting sentiments, and of establishing a chain or line of intelligence."[6]

{10} The assertion by historian Leon Litwack that "The Postmaster General's warning aroused sufficient alarm to spur legislative action"[7] seems, however, a bit exaggerated, since eight years elapsed before action took place. Nevertheless, in 1810 Congress did act. At a time when the bulk of the postal service was carried on by private contractors, and when there existed virtually no machinery by which the federal government could enforce its decrees, the legislation provided "That no other than a free white person shall be employed in carrying the mail of the United States" and that for every violation the contractor should "forfeit and pay the sum of fifty dollars; one moiety thereof to the use of the United States and the other moiety thereof to the person who shall sue for and prosecute the same."

This general prohibition was re-enacted without discussion in 1825. However, by a ruling of Postmaster General John McLean, made in 1828, Negroes were permitted to carry mailbags from stagecoach to post office, if they worked under white supervision. A re-enactment of the general mail statutes in 1863 did not repeat the prohibition, but the language of the general repealer clause of the codification left it in force. An attempt to repeal the clause passed the Senate in 1883, but the measure was tabled in the House at the urging of the Postmaster General. Not until 1865 was the prohibition

---

[5] Leon Litwack, *North of Slavery* (*Chicago:* University of Chicago Press, 1961), pp. 31, 49. See also Scott v. Sanford, 19 Howard 393 (1857) at 419.

[6] *American State Papers, Documents, Legislative and Executive* (88 vols., 1832-1861), Class VIE Post Office, p. 27. Cited by Litwack, *North of Slavery*, p. 58.

[7] Litwack, *North of Slavery*, p. 58.

formally repealed.[8]

Even in those northern states in which the Negro was granted suffrage and it was by no means a uniform practice—Negro service in public life before the Civil War, except as messenger or laborer, was nonexistent. Travelers like Sir Charles Lyell pointed to this situation, and southern leaders noted the inconsistency, the dual standard of northern spokesmen. "Sir," Calhoun's protégé Senator Butler observed in 1850, "these men repudiate the discrimination here when it suits their purpose to assail the South, but they preserve it at home.... The black man is put in a much higher scale by their rhetoric than he is by their practice."[9]

After the admission of Maine in 1820 until the end of the Civil War every new state limited the suffrage to whites,[10] In New Jersey, Connecticut, {11} New York, and Pennsylvania legal restrictions were adopted, without serious challenge. Only in Rhode Island was a restriction rescinded in that era.

The example of New York is of interest. There in the pre-Civil War period freed Negro slaves held the balance of political power. This critical role was particularly felt in elections of state legislators from New York City because of the concentration of Negro votes there; yet no enduring advantage for the Negro resulted. On the contrary, the efforts of both major parties were consistently aimed at reducing the Negro vote rather than wooing it. In 1811 the New York Democrats were able to limit Negro suffrage by a new statute requiring written proof of freedom as a condition for voting. In the celebrated convention of 1821—generally considered as the expression of the most populistic sentiments of the Democratic Jacksonian movement—enlargement of the suffrage and elimination of property qualifications for white voters were accompanied by the establishment of discriminatory property and other qualifications, that drastically reduced the Negro vote.[11] In subsequent years 1846, 1860, and 1869, the voters rejected efforts to grant equality of representation and eliminate discrimination. Only with the passage of the Fifteenth Amendment a development strongly objected to by New York Copperheads— was the restrictive provision effectively eliminated from the New York Constitution.

Ohio, Illinois, Nebraska, and the District of Columbia also considered and formally rejected Negro suffrage during the 1860's, at the height of

---

[8] *Ibid.*, pp. 58-59, Act of April 30, 1810, Ch. 54, Section 4, 2 Stat 592, 594; repeated in act of March 3, 1825, Ch. 64, Section 7, 4 Stat 104; not repeated in act of March 3, 1863, 12 Stat 701; and repealed act of March 3, 1865, 13 Stat 515.

[9] *Congressional Globe*, Thirty-First Congress, First Session, September 11, 1850, Appendix, p. 1654.

[10] The early charters and laws made no mention of race and voting. The earliest action came in 1715. Stephen B. Weeks, "The History of Negro Suffrage in the South," *Political Science Quarterly*, 9: 671 (1894).

[11] D. R. Fox, "The Negro Vote in Old New York," *Political Science Quarterly*, 32:252 (1917).

The Negro and Federal Service Before World War II

Reconstruction fervor.[12] Negro suffrage remained a central issue in presidential elections throughout the latter part of the nineteenth century.

Where suffrage was granted to Negroes, their effective use of ballot power became evident in the post-Civil War era. Elected Negro representatives sought patronage, and Negro political leaders—many of them surprisingly skillful political operators—demanded their share of the political spoils. The Negro was alert to the advantages of public office and for a number of reasons sought representation in the public service. For one thing, positions in it carried a social status few Negroes {12} could otherwise expect to achieve. Through public office Negroes could move up socially in a manner otherwise almost universally denied to those who had not had specialized or professional training. Then, too, public office was the logical next step after the franchise. Election of Negroes to public office was an important assertion of the general principle of equality and appointment to public civil office was another. Indeed as Negro suffrage was eliminated in the South after Reconstruction and representation through election declined, the importance of appointive office for Negroes was emphasized more and more by their leaders. From the beginning Negro yearbooks and reference works emphasized and took great pride—perhaps excessive pride—in even minor appointments in the public service. In the early years of the twentieth century when the Negroes' political status was perhaps at its lowest point, some of these efforts at recounting Negro achievement approach the pathetic.

The first opportunity for a Negro appointment came in the course of a maneuver by Andrew Johnson, apparently a prelude to an effort to eliminate Secretary of War Edwin Stanton from the Cabinet. Through William. Slade, a confidant of President Johnson's, the great Negro leader Frederick Douglass, born a slave, was approached with a proposal that he accept appointment to head the Freedman's Bureau. Recognizing what was at stake, that acceptance by a Negro Radical of a major post would dilute criticism of dismissal of Stanton, the leading Radical in the Cabinet, Douglass refused. Among other aspects the incident is noteworthy for the fact that Secretary of the Navy Gideon Welles absolutely opposed the appointment of any Negro to any position in the federal government, though agreeing that if "a colored person" had to be appointed the Freedman's Bureau was as good a place to put him as any.[13]

When Douglass campaigned for Grant in the following election he did so fully expecting a major appointment later. However, he was not to be the first Negro to hold a federal position. Instead Ebenezer Bassett was appointed minister to Haiti in April 1889, and a letter purporting to be a refusal of the

---

[12] Litwack, *North of Slavery*, p. 31, n. 3; J. A. Hamilton, *Negro Suffrage and Congressional Representation* (New York: Winthrop Press, 1910), pp. 22-23.

[13] Phillip S. Foner, editor, *The Life and Writings of Frederick Douglass*, Vol. IV (New York: International, 1955), pp. 33-34.

post by Douglass was made public, perhaps at the instigation of the successful candidate. Bassett is generally considered the first Negro officeholder in the federal service.

{13} Subsequently, Douglass was sent to Santo Domingo as assistant secretary to an ad hoc commission. (As he was returning to Washington from his mission, Douglass was subjected to discriminatory treatment—the captain of the Potomac mail packet denied him admission to the dining room—but he chose to make no issue of it.) Later, through political influence, he was made president of the Freedman's Bank. The latter, in spite of its name, was not strictly speaking a governmental institution but a private enterprise that was on its last legs financially and by no means free of scandal. This position was no great patronage reward.

It was not until President Hayes chose to end Reconstruction in the South that significant Negro appointments to the federal service were made, obviously as compensatory measures. Hayes's southern policy was dictated by his notion that the withdrawal of troops might facilitate a coalition of Negroes and the old Whigs into a respectable Republican party. His motives were hardly racist; the effects of his policy, as we now know, were. Revisionists in recent years have tended to blame Hayes less than early historians did; indeed it has been emphatically suggested that had Grant intelligently followed a similar policy earlier or had Johnson had a consistent southern policy, Hayes would not have been faced with Hobson's choice.[14]

In any case Hayes sought through patronage to forestall some of the wrath he feared Negroes would express in reaction to withdrawal of armed protection for them. Positions were found for displaced Negro members of southern legislatures.[15] Douglass was made marshal of the District of Columbia, a highly remunerative and very honorific position, if not a sinecure. Douglass' biographer Phillip Foner defends the Negro leader's acceptance of the post, pointing out that Douglass continued to criticize Hayes's southern policy; but C. Vann Woodward trenchantly observes that the acceptance of federal appointments by Douglass and Carl Schurz, the leader of the white Radicals, almost completely disarmed Negro opposition. In effect, concludes Woodward, {14} Douglass retired to a "twenty-one room house in the suburbs of Washington" in return for Negro acceptance of the end of Reconstruction.[16]

---

[14] See, for examples of the indictment of Johnson, L. C. Cox and. H. Cox, *Politics, Principle and Prejudice 1865-1886* (*New* York: Free Press, 1963), and Kenneth Stampp, *The Era of Reconstruction* (New York: Knopf, 1965) see, on Grant, Eli Ginzberg and Alfred S. Eichner, *The Troublesome Presence: American Democracy and the Negro* (New York: Free Press, 1964); see, on Hayes, Stanley Hirshson, *Farewell to the Bloody Shirt* (Bloomington: Indiana University Press, 1982).

[15] Vincent P. De Santis, *Republicans Face the Southern Question* (Baltimore: Johns Hopkins Press, 1959), pp. 90-91.

[16] Foner, *Douglass*, Vol. IV, p. 100; C. Vann Woodward, *Reunion and Reaction*, 2nd edition, revised (New York: Doubleday, 1950), pp. 232-283.

The Negro and Federal Service Before World War II

Douglass became a fixture of Republican administrations, though shifted from position to position, Garfield made him recorder of deeds, a minor but nonetheless lucrative post. (No less a personage than Mark Twain intervened on Douglass' behalf.) Even Cleveland retained Douglass in office for a year, as the Democratic party hesitated briefly in its attitude toward Negroes in the first months of his administration. When Harrison returned the Republicans to office, Douglass was again appointed, this time as consul general to Haiti. Harrison also appointed Negro postmasters and a Negro collector of the port of Galveston, the latter over objections from his Secretary of the Treasury.[17]

Indeed the Republicans developed a tradition of appointing Negroes to a number of minor administrative positions in the District of Columbia and diplomatic positions in countries deemed Negroid—the ministries at Liberia, Santo Domingo, and Haiti particularly. As the fundamental social consequences of Republican nonsupport for Negro rights in the South became more apparent, the number of such appointments actually increased slightly and the tradition of token Negro appointments became stronger. To the time of Wilson's inauguration some fifty Negroes held visible federal positions.[18]

In the South, however, the consequence of the new attitude condoning white supremacy was an increasingly serious loss of opportunity for Negroes to hold public office. The extent of Negro control in the South even at the apex of Reconstruction has been exaggerated by the "Vindicator" historians. For example, in Mississippi the Radical constitutional convention of 1888, the high point of Negro power in that state, compromised with regard to both prohibition on intermarriage and segregation in the schools, leaving it to the legislature to decide these issues. The Mississippi Republican ticket that year had only one Negro listed for any office, and that was for secretary of state. No Negro in any state ever held the office of governor, and only one acted temporarily as governor. In Mississippi only one Negro served as mayor and only {15} a dozen as sheriff.[19] With Hayes's withdrawal of troops, what power the Negro bad acquired receded quickly. In Georgia, for example, the legislature refused to admit duly elected Negro legislators on the grounds that the Fifteenth Amendment forbade discrimination only in voting, not in officeholding.

In their few years of officeholding in the South, Negroes did develop an amazing effectiveness in political maneuver and some achieved national prominence. For example, B. K. Bruce of Mississippi, a Republican, educated at Oberlin, was suggested for Garfield's Cabinet and was supported by Sena-

---

[17] De Santis, *Republicans Face the Southern Question*, p. 223.

[18] K. L. Wolgemuth, "Woodrow Wilson's Appointment Policy and the Negro," *Journal of Southern History*, 24: 458 (1958).

[19] V. L. Wharton, *The Negro in Mississippi, 1865-1890* (Chapel Hill: University of North Carolina Press, 1947), pp. 150, 154, 167, 169.

tor L. Q. C. Lamar and other Democrats. In some areas Negroes managed to preserve their influence until just after the beginning of the twentieth century. But in general there was a steady decline in Negro officeholding.

Some Negro officeholders took defeat bitterly, and many of the more prominent abandoned the region entirely. George H. White, the last Negro Reconstruction congressman as well as the last Negro member of the North Carolina legislature, moved to Philadelphia. John R. Lynch, a Republican congressman from Mississippi, lost his seat in 1876, regained it, but was finally defeated in a bid for re-election in 1882. After refusing several proffered appointments under Democratic administrations as a reward for silence, he wrote perhaps the first revisionist history of Reconstruction. Eventually he also migrated, and years later emerged as a political force in Chicago.

While Hayes continued during his administration to appoint Negroes to federal offices, he withdrew support from local Negro parties such as those of Bruce in Mississippi, Robert B. Elliott in South Carolina, and C. C. Antoine in Louisiana. The last in particular found himself in dire straits personally; nonetheless, the President refused to respond to his appeals for help. Hayes's bland assurances that his southern program was experimental and would be reversed in case of its failure to serve the interests of all concerned were sufficiently persuasive to hold the loyalty of northern Negroes, but these assurances proved to be largely window dressing when failure actually occurred.[20]

The Democrats on the whole failed to make appeals to the Negro and continued to reflect intransigent southern attitudes toward Negro rights. This made it easy for the Republicans to carry through in their {16} efforts to placate southern whites without losing the support of Negro voters. Arthur openly criticized Negroes for their inability to retain office and preferred to appoint whites, as "Negro officials do not help the party as much as white officials,"[21] Cleveland actually appointed more northern Negroes to offices, including some in Indiana, than his Republican predecessors, but at the same time there was a reduction in the appointments in the. South.[22] The Democrats never made a serious commitment to Negro rights, and those Negro leaders who flirted with the Democrats briefly in the 1890's quickly returned to the Republican fold.[23] Upon regaining power under McKinley, the Republican party maintained the general policy of Negro appointments established by

---

[20] De Santis, *Republicans Face the Southern Question*, pp. 130-131.

[21] Hirshson, *Farewell to the Bloody Shirt*, p. 107.

[22] Emma Lou Thornbrough, *The Negro in Indiana* (Indianapolis: Indiana Historical Bureau, 1957), pp. 301-302.

[23] August Meir, *Negro Thought in America* (Ann Arbor: University of Michigan Press, 1984), p. 34.

The Negro and Federal Service Before World War II

Hayes, though thereafter such appointments were made at a somewhat more moderate rate.

The national decline of sympathy for civil rights was most decisively reflected in Negro officeholding at the local level. During Reconstruction, Negroes occupied local offices in southern states in reasonable numbers, though by no means with strong control. In his definitive study of Reconstruction in Mississippi, V. L. Wharton accepts Lynch's conclusion that 5 percent, at most, of all county officials were Negroes. Nor did they ever have a majority in either house of the legislature. Wharton also suggests, incidentally, that more money was embezzled by Mississippi Democrats even during the Reconstruction period than by comparable Negro or white Republican officeholders.[24] Negro office-holding quickly disappeared under persistent attacks from the Vindicators who reasserted white control. In general, force and violence were the major tools of the Vindicators. Two Negro sheriffs in Mississippi were run out of office by force. Of sixteen Negro members of the 1868 constitutional convention in that state, one was hanged by the Ku Klux Klan and a second—said to be absolutely without fear—was assassinated.[25]

Negro leaders continued to wield influence in Mississippi especially through their affiliation and friendship with Senator Lamar,[26] and in {17} South Carolina mainly through the fulfilling of promises made to Negroes in return for their support of Governor Wade Hampton's campaign against the Populists. At least 86 Negroes were appointed to minor posts in South Carolina by Hampton through the 1870's and 1880's; these positions included none, however, that conceivably might be considered "major." As late as 1889 Hamptonite Governor J. P. Richardson expressed the "moderate" philosophy that "we believe that the whites must dominate but at the same time we do not refuse local offices to the blacks." Charleston and Orangeburg counties regularly had Negro legislators until 1892 and 1890 respectively. In addition some Negroes served as postmasters during the period.[27]

In northern states like Massachusetts the decline in number of officeholders, though not as great as in the South, was very revealing.[28] Kenneth Stampp suggests that as immigration became an issue in the North, ethnic prejudices and stereotypes similar in function and form to anti-Negro sentiments made northerners generally more prejudiced, less receptive to the claims of Negroes to office generally, and more willing to allow the southern

---

[24] Wharton, *The Negro in Mississippi*, pp. 189, 178, 179.

[25] *Ibid.*, pp. 147-148.

[26] *Ibid.*, pp. 180-164.

[27] George B. Tindall, *South Carolina Negroes, 1877-1900* (Columbia: University of South Carolina Press, 1952), pp. 22, 88, 39, 65.

[28] Meir, *Negro Thought in America*, p. 163.

white to deal with the Negro on his own terms.[29]

As the nineteenth century drew to a close Negro hopes hit bottom. Gradually Negroes were eliminated as senators, then as congressmen from the Deep South, and finally as representatives from the border states as well. In 1901 George H. White of North Carolina dramatically intoned his departure from Congress: "This, Mr. Chairman, is perhaps the negroes' temporary farewell to the American Congress; but let me say, Phoenix-like he will rise up some day and come again. These parting words are in behalf of an outraged, heart-broken, bruised, and bleeding, but God-fearing people.... I am pleading for the life, the liberty, the future happiness, and manhood suffrage for one-eighth of the entire population of the United States."[30]

II

Under William Howard Taft the tendency of the Roosevelt administration to minimize Negro appointments in the South was made overt {18} policy. Taft unequivocally came out against such appointments as dangerous to racial tranquility: "There is no constitutional right in anyone to hold office. The question is one of fitness. A one-legged man would hardly be selected for a mail carrier, and although we would deplore his misfortune, nevertheless we would not seek to neutralize it by giving him a place that he could not fill."[31] Inasmuch as appointment of Negroes to prominent positions in the South would create antagonism that would hamper their effectiveness, Taft chose to regard Negroes as not fit for such offices and avoided their selection. This policy largely ended the practice of appointing Negroes to postmaster-ships and other managerial positions in the South, even though their claims to these offices were stronger in that region—by virtue of their numbers—than elsewhere, Booker T. Washington was to write the President that he took it "in good spirit" and Roosevelt when he heard of the formalization of the policy said, "this is first-rate."[32] Taft did appoint William H. Lewis as Assistant Attorney General, the highest policy position achieved by a Negro to that date, but he also allowed establishment of segregation in the Census Bureau, setting a precedent to be followed in other agencies during Wilson's administration.[33]

With the elimination of Negroes as an important voting force in the

---

[29] Stampp, *The Era of Reconstruction*, pp. 19-21.

[30] *Congressional Record*, Fifty-Sixth Congress, Second Session, January 29, 1901, p. 1638.

[31] Henry Pringle, *The Life and Times of William Howard Taft* (New York: Farrar and Rinehart, 1989), p. 390.

[32] *Ibid.*

[33] *Segregation in Washington* (Chicago: National Commission on Segregation in the Nation's Capitol, n.d.), p. 80.

The Negro and Federal Service Before World War II

South—and this had been largely accomplished by the turn of the century—their leverage for obtaining patronage became negligible. Such small influence as the Negro community still had was exercised mainly through the "black and tan" parties in the South. These were largely paper organizations, but they sent delegates to the Republican national conventions who could use their votes to bargain for concessions, These delegates could hardly hope to achieve any major social advantage for their race since they were without any representation in the halls of Congress and totally lacked means of enforcing agreements reached at conventions, Consequently they primarily sought whatever personal advantage could be gained and occasionally persuaded party leaders to adopt platform statements, conveniently abstract, with regard to Negro rights. But even these were to decline in specificity and frequency in Republican platforms as Negro voter {19} strength in the South steadily diminished and the building of a "lily white" Republican party in the South came to seem the only sensible policy. After 1908, indeed, the major Republican platform provision on civil rights was advocacy of an anti-lynch law, a comparatively unobjectionable position.

On the whole political patronage had proved an inadequate means to expanded Negro opportunity. It was rather the civil service, with its merit system, that opened the way to Negro participation in public life.

The establishment of the classified civil service in 1885 placed some 14,000 government positions under this system. At the time of adoption of the Pendleton Act it was estimated that there were 620 Negroes employed by the government in Washington, D.C.[34] In 1892 the Civil Service Commission found that there were 2,393 Negro employees in Washington. Statistics of this period have questionable validity; but the general impression remains that the growth of Negro civil service was sustained, vigorous, and definite at least until the early years of the Wilson administration.

In his authoritative history of the civil service, Van Riper follows the suggestion of Laurence J. W. Hayes that the Wilson administration impeded Negro employment in the bureaucracy. To support this, Van Riper utilizes data from Hayes's study indicating a decline in the proportion of Negroes in the federal service from nearly 6 percent in 1910 to 4.9 percent in 1918.[35] Examination of Hayes's data, however, reveals that virtually the entire "decline"—from 5.86 percent in 1910 to 4.98 percent in 1912—would have had to take place during the Taft years, which Hayes regards as advantageous for mass Negro employment. It is obvious that the "decline" is largely an artifact

---

[34] Laurence J. W. Hayes, *The Negro Federal Government Worker: A Study of His Classification Status in the District of Columbia, 1883-1988* (Washington, D.C.: Howard University Graduate School, 1941), p. 19. Although there are obvious contradictions in it, this study remains the basic point of departure for analysis of this subject.

[35] Paul Van Riper, *History of the United States Civil Service* (Evanston, Ill.: Row, Peterson, 1958), p. 242.

THE NEGRO IN FEDERAL EMPLOYMENT

of using non-comparable estimates from quite different sources. Hayes's figures for the 1912-1918 period show an increase in absolute numbers of 25,000 Negro employees and a minor decline in the proportion of Negroes in the bureaucracy. (Hayes summarizes this as a decline from 4.98 percent to 4.90 percent; his raw data suggest an even less significant {20} drop to 4.94 percent in 1918.[36]) In short the figures available suggest the possibility that there was an actual decline in the early Wilson years, but in view of the crudity of the figures, we do not seem justified in accepting this as fact. It is clear that there was some decline in "major appointments"—a white man was appointed minister to Haiti, for example; the total pattern, however, is problematic. Nonetheless, it seems fair to label the period from 1913 to 1921, as does Van Riper, "the most critical period in the recent history of Negro federal civil service employment."[37] Certainly if there was no actual decline under the Wilson administration it was not due to the policies of the President and his subordinates.

Secretary of the Treasury McAdoo and Postmaster General Burleson established a policy of segregation and Wilson was to write of the actions of his son-in-law, "I would say that I do approve of segregation that is being attempted in several of the departments." The President further indicated his personal belief in segregation of the races by attending a private showing of *The Birth of a Nation*. Wilson also appointed many fewer than the traditional fifty or so Negroes to various minor administrative posts.[38]

It should be noted, however, that the administration had been under considerable pressure from the Congress to establish such a policy. The appointment of an Oklahoma Negro, A. E. Patterson, as register of the Treasury failed to obtain confirmation in the Senate; eventually his name was withdrawn. Simultaneously, bills were introduced in the Congress to compel segregation in the federal service and to prohibit the appointment of any Negro as the superior of any Caucasian. The latter proposal was defended by its sponsor, James B. Aswell, a representative from Louisiana: "The Almighty by the stamp of color decreed that the Caucasian race should occupy positions of authority and control the destinies of this country.... If we would be just to each race we would recognize the eternal fitness of things in this Government as did Lincoln and Jefferson. We would know that this is a white man's country whose future is to be controlled by the Caucasian race. It is {21} unjust to a member of this inferior race to put him in positions of authority...

---

[36] Hayes, *The Negro Federal Government Worker*, p. 153. See also the confirming estimate in Kelly Miller, *Segregation: The Caste System and the Civil Service* (N.p.: published by the author, 1914(?)), p. 7.

[37] Van Riper, *History of the United States Civil Service*, p. 242.

[38] Arthur Link, *Wilson: The New Freedom* (Princeton, N.J.: Princeton University Press, 1958), pp. 248-253.

even over his own race."[39]

Not only were these extreme proposals defeated, but the public outcry at them and at establishment of segregation in the Navy caused some mitigation of the new policies of segregation, though not their elimination, Indeed for the first time the federal service was recognizing officially the institution of segregation. Previously the pattern had been much more vague, although discrimination and segregation had undoubtedly been practiced from time to time. Now the public outcry helped underscore the fact that the full weight of an administration was clearly furthering the "caste system," as Kelly Miller pointed out in an anguished pamphlet of 1914.[40]

While there was some strategic retreat in segregation policies as a result of public pressure, social practices had been introduced that were to persist. Additionally, changes in civil service regulations had far-reaching results, On May 27, 1914, the Civil Service Commission introduced the requirement that a photograph be attached to applications for government jobs. As Van Riper writes, "Whether or not this change was directed solely at Negro applicants for public office is not absolutely certain."[41] The timing, however, is highly suggestive.[42] An application photograph has many uses; determination of color is only one possibility. But when supervisors by the "rule of three" were given the power of selecting among candidates, the photograph proved a potent weapon for discrimination.

Segregation policies were partially offset by the advent of World War I; considerable Negro gains were made during the war, particularly at higher level positions. But the end of the war saw a cutback in total employment and a shift in the pattern of Negro employment. Further, the impact of the segregation policies was widely felt; the Navy, for example, had required its Negro clerks to do their work behind screens.

{22} Under Republican administrations, beginning with Harding's, there was a rise in sheer numbers of Negro employees through the 1920's. As early as 1928 Negroes were estimated to constitute 15 to 30 percent of postal workers in major local post offices.[43] (The long tradition of Negro service in the Post Office Department, with accumulated seniority buttressed by orga-

---

[39] *Segregation of Clerks and Employees in the Civil Service*, Hearings before the Commission on Reform in the Civil Service (House of Representatives), Sixty-Third Congress, Second Session, 1914 (Washington, D.C.: Government Printing Office, 1914), p. 3.

[40] *Segregation: The Caste System and the Civil Service.*

[41] Van Riper, *History of the United States Civil Service*, pp. 241-242.

[42] For some standard criticisms by Negro leaders, see the comments of Congressman Mitchell, who opposed putting postmasters under civil service, which he characterized as representing "hypocrisy and absolute unfairness." *Congressional Record*, Appendix, Seventy-Fifth Congress, Second Session, December 15,1937, p. 478-477.

[43] Sterling Spero and Abram Harris, *The Black Worker* (New York: Columbia University Press, 1931), p. 122.

nized power in the form of Negro postal workers unions and outside groups, is just beginning in the 1980's to pay off in terms of promotion and status for nonwhites.) By 1928 the percentage of Negroes in the federal service as a whole was estimated as 9.59,[44] representing almost a doubling from the beginning of the Republican era in 1921.

In the 1920's the Secretary of Commerce, Herbert Hoover, drew fire from southern congressmen for desegregating the Census Bureau and effecting other changes to enforce non-discrimination. In addition, various offices in the departments of Commerce, Interior, and Treasury were also in part desegregated, leading to accusations of "delegate buying" by Deep South Senators Blease and Heflin.[45]

III

There was little indication in 1932 that the New Deal would emerge as a major friend of the Negroes. The Democratic platform of that year is devoid of reference to civil rights; this had been standard practice in Democratic platforms. (The most conspicuous mention of equal rights in the previous years of the Democratic party was the 1888 plank identifying that concept with the abolition of the Freedman's Bureau and other signs of "Negro supremacy"! Most Democratic platforms had scrupulously avoided the issue.) Further, Franklin Delano Roosevelt had served as Assistant Secretary of the Navy in Wilson's administration and was thus associated with the most infamous discriminatory measures instituted in the federal service.

But the New Deal certainly opened opportunities to Negroes, though in spotty fashion. Its impact was not nearly so great in sheer numbers of jobs provided as in level of service opened up. It is estimated that the percentage of Negroes in the service rose only slightly, to 9.85 percent {23} in 1938.[46] Also, discrimination on the job did continue—the CCC for example was bitterly criticized by Negro leaders as particularly oppressive in that it introduced discriminatory practices among youth—but significant inroads were made too. Harold Ickes in the Interior Department, for instance, ended segregated lunchroom facilities for his Washington employees,[47] and he is

---

[44] Hayes, *The Negro Federal Government Worker*, p. 153.

[45] *Congressional Record*, Seventieth Congress, First Session, April 16, 1928, pp. 6486-6487; May 3, 1928, pp. 7698-7702.

[46] Van Riper, *History of the United States Chit Service*, p. 242; but the raw figures in his source, Hayes, *The Negro Federal Government Worker*, p. 153, compute to 9.5 percent, compared with nearly 9.6 percent a decade earlier. It appears likely that the summary estimates are more accurate than the estimates of actual figures.

[47] In many departments before World War II there were two lunchrooms, one large and one small, which serviced white and Negro employees respectively. In the 1940's and 1950's, when integration became the universal pattern for governmental employment, the smaller units in many instances were converted into executive dining rooms. In one of those small

The Negro and Federal Service Before World War II

generally credited with inaugurating the practice of bringing in Negro professionals as "consultants" or special assistants.

Ickes had served as an official of the National Association for the Advancement of Colored People, and while he was fearless in his advocacy of non-discrimination throughout his department he saw no hope of ending segregation entirely and was not inclined to waste time in pursuing unattainable goals. On the other hand, as he noted in his *Diary*, when there were complaints about working with Negro superiors he consistently responded: "I will not stand for racial discrimination and I have stood against it from the first." If the employee "felt he could not work on courteous *terms* with a Negro, I would be very glad to accept his resignation."[48] Many of the New Deal projects were overtly segregated or followed discriminatory practices, however, even in the Interior Department.

But the basic New Deal programs of social amelioration created a logic and a moral dimension of their own. The intervention of federal authority in new areas suggested new social patterns as well. White humanitarian Will Alexander, then active in the Rosenwald Fund and ancillary activities, sensed this early in the Roosevelt administration. He quickly convinced Edwin K. Embree, president of the Fund, that "the next stage in improvement of race relations in the country would probably center around events in Washington. As men interested in {24} securing such improvement, they should go to Washington and see somebody.'"[49]

With Embree and Charles Johnson of Fiske University, Alexander decided there was a need for a Negro in the federal administration who would act as a spokesman for equal rights. They determined that it would be better to have him working within the administrative structure rather than functioning as a mere lobbyist, but with a salary from outside sources. Securing White House approval, the trio then set out to find a place for such an individual. They first considered the Department of Labor where there was already a young North Carolina Negro employed, But since Embree knew Ickes they decided to approach instead the Secretary of the Interior, who they believed would be resolute in his support for such a person if he approved of the idea, After consideration Ickes agreed to appoint a Negro as a special adviser in his department, and a list of a half dozen names was submitted to him, together with assurances that the salary would be paid by the Rosenwald Fund. Typically, Ickes selected the one who was last on their list and in their judgment least likely to be politically acceptable, though highly competent: Clark Fore-

---

but gratifying bits of historic irony, I was able to secure admittance to one of these inner sanctums by lunching with and interviewing a Negro colleague, now a governmental executive.

[48] *The Secret Diary of Harold Ickes*, Vol. III (New York: Simon and Schuster, 1953), p. 641.

[49] Dykeman and James Stokely, *Seeds of Southern Change: The Life of Will Alexander* (Chicago: University of Chicago Press, 1962), p. 193.

man, a young Negro with little experience and very positive convictions. Foreman shortly thereafter secured as his assistant Robert C. Weaver, who was, of course, to have his own independent successful career.

The initial hope had been that a man placed in the Interior Department could have an influence throughout the governmental structure. Foreman quickly found that working across departmental lines was extremely difficult. The best that could be hoped for really was to inculcate by example, to show the advantages of top-level Negro service, When Foreman left for another position, Weaver moved up to succeed him. Soon other advisers were added, like William Hastie, also in Interior, and Mrs. Mary McLeod Bethune, in the National Youth Administration; the group came to be called the "Black Cabinet" and engendered considerable criticism, some of it from Negro sources, The principal responsibility of the group was to provide guidance on interracial issues for administration leaders and to assist with minority group patronage, leading one critic to dub them the "porkbarrelencis africanus." In time Negroes came to resent very much these positions {25} of non-responsibility and solely symbolic recognition in the federal service. For example, Ralph Bunche in a memo to the Republican National Committee in 1939 indicated that such honorific positions "mean a salary for the officeholders... but are of no significance to the welfare of the Negro... there is in consequence, growing lack of respect for the Negro officeholder in the federal government" He saw the practice of appointing advisers as perhaps an improvement over the traditional spoils system but noted that "in no single instance has the Negro been appointed to a really responsible policy-forming position in the Government."[50]

In their day, however, these positions constituted a breakthrough and John Hope Franklin, the distinguished Negro historian, concluded that "while the 'Black Cabineteers' were not responsible for all of the improvements of the conditions of Negro federal employees, they could view with pride all of the changes and could claim as their handiwork a considerable number of them."[51] The presence of the Negroes in at least nominally important positions of high status constituted in itself an attack upon entrenched social

---

[50] Ralph Bunche, "Report on the Needs of the Negro for the Republican Program Committee" (unpublished manuscript, July 1, 1939, Schomburg Collection, New York Public Library), p. 124. See also Bunche, "The Political Status of the Negro" (unpublished manuscript, Carnegie Myrdal Study, September 1940, Schomburg Collection, New York Public Library).

[51] John Hope Franklin, *From Slavery to Hope*, 2nd edition, revised (New York: Knopf, 1980), p. 522. As early as 1934, Congressman Gavagan listed the following Negroes in administrative positions: Eugene Kinckle Jones, Special Services, Department of Commerce; Forester B. Washington and Earl R. Moses, Federal Emergency Relief; Robert L. Vann, Special Assistant Attorney General; William H. Hastie and Theophilus Mann, Department of the Interior; H. D. Hunt, Farm Credit Administration; T. M. Campbell and J. B. Pierce, Department of Agriculture; Lawrence A. Oxley, Department of Labor. *Congressional Record*, Seventy-Third Congress, Second Session, June 18, 1934, pp. 12607-12609.

The Negro and Federal Service Before World War II

customs throughout the public service. The presence of spokesmen helped translate into practice the principle—which made great advances under the New Deal that opportunity should not be limited by race. Thus, the benefits of many relief programs and other federal government services were made available for Negro citizens on a level, approaching equality with that for whites. Need, after all, was the overriding standard that could be continuously referred to in countering discrimination and could be invoked effectively by those within an administrative structure.

With the appointment of such people throughout the bureaucracy, and with the announcement of a social program of real import to the average {26} Negro voter, the Democrats for the first time had potent arguments to use in persuading Negroes to break away from their traditional Republican affiliations. The *Congressional Record* provides evidence that Democrats were aware of the possibilities of winning Negro voters. In 1933, 1934, and 1936 speeches were made on the topic of Negro appointments to civil service positions. While these bear witness to progress, they also give clear evidence of the limits of amelioration. For example, on June 18, 1934, Congressman Joseph Gavagan, who represented Harlem at the time, in describing the contributions of the New Deal to the cause of the Negro cited specifically the use of Negro elevator operators in the Washington Post Office, presumably for the first time, and in the Commerce Building. He took these examples to indicate that great strides had been made toward equal opportunity in the federal service.[52] Washington obviously was still a heavily segregated city with little opportunity for the Negro; as Will Alexander pointed out, "In Washington itself, one could work all day in a government building and hardly see a Negro until five o'clock when the colored cleaning women came to sweep and dust."[53]

In 1934 the congressional restaurant remained basically segregated. The basement grillroom was reserved for Negroes, with slightly cheaper prices charged for the same food.[54] When Congressman Oscar DePriest of Illinois complained because some Negro students were turned away from the main restaurant, it was argued that this was a long-established custom. DePriest himself had been accorded the full privileges of the main restaurant, and these would be extended to his guests, it was explained. (Even this represented a distinct advance; when DePriest came to the Congress in 1929 Speaker Longworth had been forced to give the oath en masse for fear there might be

---

[52] Even more disingenuously he noted that 28 of the 52 "White House employees" were colored. *Congressional Record*, Seventy-Third Congress, Second Session, June 18, 1934, pp. 12607-12608.

[53] Dykeman and Stokely, *Seeds of Southern Change*, p. 194.

[54] *Congressional Record*, Seventy-Third Congress, Second Session, March 21 and 23, 1934, pp, 5048, 5255.

some abuse of the congressman.[55]) But as to the efforts to secure equal access to the restaurant for all, the North Carolina congressman who was chairman of the supervisory committee objected, explaining that he was "as free from racial and religious intolerance as any man in this House," but that {27} efforts to end the traditional policy were the tactics of "a mob of toughs and hoodlums from Howard University" who were Socialists and worse.[56]

Although numerically the New Deal advances were relatively slight, and not particularly distinguishable from the advances made under the Republican administrations of the 1920's, the percentage of Negroes in the federal service was slowly inching toward a level commensurate with the percentage of nonwhites in the general populace. In the late years of the New Deal the proportion of Negroes in the federal service apparently reached the nonwhite proportion of the general population. But not all the New Deal was advantageous to the Negro. The NRA—perhaps the most adventurous New Deal program—was a disaster for Negro workers: decentralized governmental planning meant jobs and other advantages went to those with local political power and Negroes were conspicuously weak in that respect.[57] Negroes welcomed relief from the effects of the NIRA when it was declared unconstitutional. Friendly attitudes among administrators seemed to produce few concrete advantages in programs or employment, public or private. But somehow it was clear that change was in the wind.

---

[55] Harold Gosnell, *Negro Politicians* (Chicago: University of Chicago Press, 1935), p. 184.

[56] *Congressional Record*, Seventy-Third Congress, Second Session, March 23,1934, p. 52-55.

[57] Ginzberg and Eichner, *The Troublesome Presence*, p. 294; Franklin, *From Slavery to Hope*, pp. 523-524.

2
The Negro and the Federal Service in an Era of Change

I

{28}
FOR the Negro, World War II marked a turning point. This period saw the confluence of a number of forces, each of which had been gathering momentum in the immediately preceding years. The scientific historians of the future will find it difficult to disentangle them and to delineate precisely which constituted the determinative forces for progress; conversely, observers with pet theories will find it easy to discover their favorite historical motif in operation. Certainly, however, the growth of Negro economic and political power, the northern migration and urbanization of Negroes, the rise in their educational level, their development of organizational techniques, the absence of competition in the labor market, and the stimulation (by the trauma of Hitlerism) of a keener sense among all Americans of the costs of racism— all played their part. For the Negro subculture of our society, something like Rostow's postulated state of "take-off" was re-enacted. The small, painful advances in the prewar years here employment of Negroes as elevator operators, there enrollment of a handful at a university or the banding together of a small group into a political organization—paved the way for a major surge when the opportunity was at hand.

Changes in perspective with regard to the civil rights movement are {29} inevitable with the passage of time. But from the vantage point of the mid-1960's, the crucial event looms large and clear—an event that indeed never took place. The planned "March on Washington" in 1941 denoted a new stage in the development of Negro militancy—the scope and substance of demand were of a different order from any earlier effort; a new stage of Negro organization—the mounting of even the threat of the march required preparation and communication to a degree never before attempted; and a new concept of Negro strategy—the discovery was made that public pressure was a weapon available to a minority community. The plan for the march was the prototype of, a rehearsal for, the more dramatic and far-reaching efforts of the 1960's; the effect it had foreshadowed the political gains of later years. The basic ingredients of future strategy—threats of international embarrassment to the United States government and of internal disruption of the domestic establishment—were tried and found potent. In addition, the Negro leadership gained maturity and self-respect and self-knowledge.

It was in January 1941 that A. Philip Randolph, head of the Brotherhood of Sleeping Car Porters, conceived of the march as a way of demonstrating the potential power of the Negro. Faced with the position of the Roosevelt administration, certainly a friendly establishment, that no further economic and social advances for the Negro could be achieved through governmental or political means during the war crisis, Negro leaders nevertheless aggressively demanded governmental protection of the right to equal employment opportunity. To enforce this demand, Randolph came up with the idea of a march on the capital. He pushed his idea for months against the cool indifference and doubts of most of the rather conservative civil rights leaders. To a large extent, as Herbert Garfinkel has shown, support for the march came from the grass roots, forcing reluctant agreement from Negro leaders.[1] Whether the widespread discontent among the Negro masses, which was a reality, could have been organized is, however, problematic. Randolph at various times predicted that 10,000, 50,000, even 100,000 marchers would converge on Washington. But the test of that ability to perform was, as it turned out, not necessary.

Enormous pressures were brought to bear upon Randolph and other {30} Negro leaders to reconsider their plan. The threat it posed for the administration was a multiple one: it suggested a dramatic exposure of racialism in a country fighting a war premised upon opposition to racism; it also threatened consequences in reactions of Negro servicemen and potential draftees, and an inevitable divisiveness in internal politics generally. Eleanor Roosevelt and Fiorello La Guardia were only two of those whose persuasiveness was enlisted in support of the administration's position and whose importunities were hard for Negro leaders to ignore. When the Negroes persisted in the face of pleas, threats, and cajolings, however, the administration itself reconsidered. It had been effectively pressured into doing what its leaders by and large felt was morally desirable but feared would prove politically embarrassing. Now it had been demonstrated that embarrassment was a two-edged blade.

On June 25, a week before the scheduled march, President Roosevelt issued Executive Order 8802 on equal employment. Only the day before, La Guardia had informed the civil rights leaders of the President's willingness to meet their demands and had worked out an agreement with them, including a specific reference to equality in government employment. The order established a Committee on Fair Employment Practice "to provide for the full and equitable participation of all workers in defense industries, without discrimination."

---

[1] Herbert Garfinkel, *When Negroes March* (Glencoe, Ill.: Free Press, 1959), pp. 39-41 and 51ff. I have drawn generally from this informative study.

II

It would be foolish to suggest that this or subsequent orders accomplished all that they purported to seek. No authority was given the Committee on Fair Employment Practice over military personnel at all.[2] As to civilian employment, the President's proclamation did not alter the situation overnight. The primary instrumentality of change with regard to the labor force was not the law of the land but the law of supply and demand. As a shortage of available manpower developed in the wake of increasing production and withdrawal from the labor force of large numbers of able-bodied men, jobs formerly closed opened {31} up to Negroes—in numbers approximating the changeover of a major revolution. At most, laws and regulations were a secondary factor in this change. The bitter opposition of southern congressmen and senators to the fair employment program for government and defense industries suggests that it was thought to have some effect on labor practices generally, but perhaps their vehement protest centered on the governmental agency as a convenient symbol.

The first Committee on Fair Employment Practice was administratively poorly conceived and understaffed.[3] Its triumphs were mainly in airing the problem of discrimination and in moral suasion. Additionally, the Civil Service Commission was induced to add clarifying provisions in its own regulations to further codify the new official stance of the government. The committee, armed with the presidential order and a supplemental letter of September 3, 1941, reached agreement with the commission by which the latter undertook investigations on behalf of the committee.[4] In November 1942 the Civil Service Commission urged all agencies to utilize its new standard form for employment, eliminating photographs.[5] Increasingly too government agencies were forced, because of the wartime shortage of labor, to rely on the Civil Service Commission as a central pool for employees, and hence the commission could place Negroes from its pool in a variety of positions.[6]

The changes in governmental service were remarkable, even against the

---

[2] *First Report, Fair Employment Practice Committee, July 1943–December 1944* (Washington, D.C.: Government Printing Office, 1945), p. 7; John A. Davis, "Nondiscrimination in the Federal Agencies," *Annals of the American Academy of Political and Social Science*, 244:65-74 (March 1946). In 1944 the committee reached agreement with the War and Navy departments controlling discrimination in war installations.

[3] Paul Van Riper, *History of the United States Civil Service* (Evanston, Ill.: Row, Peterson, 1958), p. 438; Davis, "Nondiscrimination in the Federal Agencies," *Annals*, 244: 69. At its peak the agency had 53 persons concerned with operations.

[4] Davis, "Nondiscrimination in the Federal Agencies," *Annals*, 244: 89.

[5] Gladys Kammerer, *Impact of War on Federal Personnel Administration, 1939-1945* (Lexington: University of Kentucky Press, 1951), p. 50n.

[6] Davis, "Nondiscrimination in the Federal Agencies," *Annals*, 244: 70.

background of changes in American society generally. Here, after all, legal regulations, when enforced by conscientious administrators, could be more influential than in the nongovernmental sector of employment. On the eve of the war, for the first time, regulations and legislation expressly prohibited racial discrimination in federal employment. As of 1940 civil service regulations explicitly forbade the use of political and religious affiliations as criteria for employment. There was, however, no mention of these being forbidden standards in promotion policy. Nor was there any mention at all of race in either context; {32} when any questions were raised the explanation usually proffered was that the merit system by implication forbade the utilization of such criteria, but logically the same argument should also have made redundant the other two prohibitions. In 1940 Congressman Robert Ramspeck of Georgia, a devoted advocate of the merit system, introduced legislation for a general revision of civil service including provisions forbidding discrimination on grounds of race. The Civil Service Commission and the President hastily acted, only nineteen days before passage of the Ramspeck Act, to promulgate anti-discrimination regulations, obviously to avoid the embarrassment of being forced by another branch of the government to outlaw race prejudice.[7] With the Executive Order of November 7, 1940, reinforced shortly by the Ramspeck Act, racial discrimination became illegal in both employment and promotion policies.

These legal changes helped bring about significant advances in the governmental service. But the general pattern of Negro employment in the less desirable positions that still characterized the economy as a whole prevailed in government too. By and large Negroes found their best opportunities for jobs in positions that whites eschewed, the hand-me-downs of employment.

An analysis made by William Chapman Bradbury in 1952 of figures supplied by the early Committee on Fair Employment Practice showed that Negro employees were concentrated in the temporary war agencies rather than in the older establishments, in less permanent positions, in the more menial roles, and in the Washington, D.C. area rather than in the field. Also, the higher the classification of a Negro, the more likely it was that he held a temporary position or was employed by a strictly wartime agency. More than half of all Negroes in classified service were in temporary positions, and half were in wartime agencies.

The concentration of Negro employment in Washington reflected not only the greater control exercised by high-level officials over the employment structure there but, even more, the general shortage of labor in that district. More detailed scrutiny bears this out rather strikingly. The dramatic rise of Negro service in Washington was not paralleled in the field where the growth was only from some 10 percent of all employees in the prewar period to 11

---

[7] Van Riper, *History of the United States Civil Service*, pp. 344-347, 438.

percent in 1944. Eighty percent {33} of the Negroes in the field were still in the unclassified service, and only 2.6 percent of all clerical and administrative positions in the field were occupied by Negroes.[8]

What was significant, however, was that Negroes in the civil service, at least in Washington, now had sufficient numbers and experience to assert their claims and maintain their role in the after-war period. There was no repetition of the post-World War I situation where Negro gains were wiped out almost overnight. From March 31, 1944, to July 31, 1947, a comparison of figures compiled for a sample group of agencies by the Committee on Fair Employment Practice with figures compiled by the President's Commission on Human Rights showed, there was a slight drop in the percentage of Negroes employed, but the basic pattern remained remarkably stable during those years, both in numbers and in distribution of Negroes in the middle reaches of the bureaucracy.[9]

The wartime committee found it was not easy to implement its theoretical powers. At first, having no field staff, the committee had to utilize the investigative resources of the Civil Service Commission. The commission cooperated freely, and the committee could pursue any investigation further if it chose. But the arrangement was less than ideal. The commission refused to intervene in questions of working conditions, work assignments, or other matters within the administrative discretion of the several agencies."[10] A Negro could not secure a position allocated to another qualified person even if discrimination had been involved in the appointment, making it of doubtful benefit to the individual to bring a complaint. "In government cases the Committee has *never been allowed* to hold public hearings as in the case of war industries, and thus the sanction of public opinion has not been open to it" (emphasis added), a leading member of the wartime committee staff wrote toward the end of its existence. "As the enforcing agent of the national nondiscrimination policy," he suggested somewhat halfheartedly, "Government would perhaps be in an unfortunate position to have to expose its failings to the public."[11] Only three governmental {34} hearings were held, of cases in the Department of Commerce, the Office of Education, and the Newport News Post Office. Nor, by its own admission, did the committee use what power it had to make general recommendations to any great extent.

In all, the Civil Service Commission investigated 1,871 complaints for the committee between October 1941 and March 1946 and found racial discrimi-

---

[8] William Chapman Bradbury, Jr., "Racial Discrimination in the Federal Service" (Ph.D. dissertation, Columbia University, 1952; University Microfilms No. 4557), pp. 40-41.

[9] *Ibid.*, pp. 44-48, concludes this from unpublished records of the Committee on Fair Employment Practice now in the National Archives. See especially his tabulation for ten permanent agencies, p. 48.

[10] Davis, "Nondiscrimination in the Federal Agencies," *Annals*, 244: 67.

[11] *Ibid.*, p. 67; *First Report, Fair Employment Practice Committee*, p. 48.

nation in only 58 instances.[12] (The commission, it should be noted, insisted on defining discrimination solely in terms of violation of its own rules.) The Committee on Fair Employment Practice itself handled 2,048 complaints against the federal government from July 1943 to June 1945, securing adjustments in 23 percent of these cases, compared with adjustments in 39 percent of all cases handled.[13] Perhaps its major function in the government employment area was the inauguration of thorough statistical studies on the extent of racial discrimination,

The modest accomplishments of the Committee on Fair Employment Practice (actually there were two committees of the same name during the wartime period, the first functioning from August 1941 until January 1943, the second beginning its term of office in May 1943[14]) must be viewed in relation to the pressure being exerted in support of the pattern of discriminatory employment. The fair employment program was always a target for congressional criticism. The quest for equality took many guises and alternate forms, in large part as a consequence of that criticism. Originally, the committee was in the Office of Production Management; later it was moved to the War Manpower Commission. Congress refused to make the agency permanent and in fact ended the committee in 1946 through the so-called Russell Amendment to an appropriations bill. The latter provided that any temporary agency was to be abolished after one year if Congress had not appropriated money for it. The action was clearly aimed at the Committee on Fair Employment Practice and was universally so understood. The following year the amendment was modified to allow the establishment of interdepartmental {35} agencies on a temporary basis, so long as the employees remained on the payrolls of the regular agencies.[15] As a consequence, in later years agencies in the fair employment field were set up as interdepartmental, temporary, executive creations. The exception was President Truman's Fair Employment Board which was set up in 1948 as part of the Civil Service Commission. Not until the Civil Rights Act of 1964 was congressional approval given to a fair employment agency.

The unfriendliness of Congress was an obstacle to the development of equal employment practices, but every President since Roosevelt has main-

---

[12] *Final Report, Fair Employment Practice Committee, June 26, 1946* (Washington, D.C.: Government Printing Office, 1947), pp. 31-32.

[13] Davis, "Nondiscrimination in the Federal Agencies," *Annals*, 244:71-72; *Final Report, Fair Employment Practice Committee*, p. 32. The committee's final report did not give comparable data for the total period of its functioning. Presumably, they would reveal a similar pattern of effectiveness, though at a lower level.

[14] Paul Norgren and Samuel Hill, *Toward Fair Employment* (New York: Columbia University Press, 1964), p. 150.

[15] U.S. Civil Rights Commission, *Employment* (Washington, D.C.: Government Printing Office, 1961), pp. 19-21.

tained such programs, Truman not only set up the Fair Employment Board but also established, in 1952, the President's Committee on Government Contract Compliance, to police the non-discrimination clause in governmental contracts, a provision required by Executive Order 9346 of 1943. A successor Committee on Government Contracts was appointed by President Eisenhower in 1953. After temporizing with a committee authorized merely to receive complaints, Eisenhower also established, on January 18, 1955, a presidential Committee on Government Employment Policy. It had only advisory powers. Many of the characteristic aspects of the fair employment program took form in the Eisenhower years. The separation of the "fair employment officer" from the personnel officer in federal agencies, for example, was an early decision, made under the assumption that a person should not function in a semi-judicial capacity after creating the situation in an executive capacity. (In Truman's administration the agency head had in most instances also been the equal employment officer.) The involvement of Vice President Richard Nixon in one aspect of the program, the Committee on Government Contracts, set another early precedent.

The defeat until 1964 of fair employment practices as a legislative program at the national level was also mitigated by the gradual development of fair employment commissions at the state level. Although by 1945 a number of states already had statutes prohibiting discrimination—thirteen, according to Theodore Leskes[16]—New York State was the first to set up machinery for enforcement, by establishing in that year a commission. Later in 1945, New Jersey created a Division {36} against Discrimination within the Department of Education. By 1966, 29 states had some rudimentary enforcement legislation.[17] These laws were of diverse effectiveness, scope, and specificity, but their mere existence was evidence of a considerable body of sentiment in favor of nondiscrimination in employment generally and, therefore, had important implications for public employment policy. Certainly it was anomalous for the public sector of employment to follow practices which were condemned as improper by the government in its supervisory capacity.

III

On March 6, 1961, President Kennedy issued Executive Order 10925 which vested the functions of both the Committee on Government Contracts and the Committee on Government Employment Policy in a new President's Committee on Equal Employment Opportunity. In a move that was calculated

---

[16] Milton Konvitz and Theodore Leskes, A *Century of Civil Rights* (New York: Columbia University Press, 1961), p. 197.

[17] States having anti-discrimination legislation and the enforcing agencies are listed in U.S. Commission on Civil Rights, *Equal Employment Opportunity under the Federal Law* (Washington, D.C.: Government Printing Office, 1966), pp. 6-10.

to enhance the liberal reputation of Vice President Johnson as well as to secure confidence in the committee, he appointed Johnson permanent chairman. The Secretary of Labor was designated vice chairman.

The order creating the new committee was far more elaborate and constructive than any previous executive order in this field. It gave the committee stronger powers than earlier committees had had, particularly in its requirement that the functions of the committee were not to be merely negative or corrective in nature, but were to be utilized for "positive compliance." The governmental fair employment program transferred to the new committee was concentrated in a separate division. The director for governmental employment throughout the life of the committee was John Hope II, a Negro scholar and administrator whose father had been president and one of the founders of Atlanta University and who, in his own right, had years of experience in the fair employment field.

Much the largest area of activity for the committee was the contract compliance program. Here differences of opinion developed between two committee members, the executive director, John Feild, and Robert Troutman, a businessman and friend of Kennedy's, over voluntary compliance for businesses. Eventually both men were to leave the committee. {37} The governmental program was, however, relatively free of personality clashes and disagreements over approach.

The pronounced emphasis upon the placing of Negroes in high-level positions is said to have started when Robert Kennedy, speaking to businessmen in Birmingham, urged them to employ Negroes and was met by some sarcastic remarks about the character of federal employment in that region. When the then Attorney General investigated he indeed found, according to this story, that the federal government was even more discriminatory than the average business in its employment practices there; he thereupon determined to correct the situation.

It was soon apparent, however, that the mere removal of barriers did not guarantee equal access to jobs. Experience with recruitment under the new federal policy in the South revealed that the earlier pattern of discrimination had itself created social patterns that remained to reinforce unequal employment practices even when a more positive attitude on the part of the administrators in power was evident.

The Kennedy program of conspicuous employment of Negroes at high-grade positions at levels previously not truly open to the Negro was hardly of an apolitical nature. The director of the minorities division of the Democratic National Committee, Louis Martin, himself a Negro and former journalist, worked closely with the White House in this program and vigorously pursued publicity for political advantage. As he frankly stated in an interview, he was consistently looking for appointments with a political impact that statistics, important as they are, could not have. "Hell, I even had a candidate for

Secretary of State," he has said.[18] In 1960 he had drawn up a list of some 750 Negroes of ability and set out to try to find employment for them; efforts to place Mexican Americans and other "nonwhites" were also made, but the most conspicuous advances were clearly in Negro employment.

Aiding Mr. Martin in the Kennedy years was Ralph Dungan of the White House staff. He was in charge of filling major staff positions throughout the bureaucracy and was therefore also involved in this effort to symbolize and dramatize the end of discrimination in the federal service. For a brief period of one year Harris Wofford, Jr., acted as White House aid on minority rights. But this did not prove successful. Lee White of the White House staff was also concerned with minority rights and gradually took over more and more of this function {38} in the later years of the Kennedy administration and in the first years of the Johnson administration.[19] Additionally, a sub-Cabinet committee of assistant secretaries met roughly once a month to coordinate activities and compare approaches to problems,

The President's Committee on Equal Employment Opportunity plugged away at compiling the day-to-day statistics and establishing the pattern for routine employment in the bureaucracy, its hand strengthened by dramatic appointments which indicated solidly that a new day had arrived. The annual census of employment which the committee initiated in 1961 provided a factual basis for discussion of the record in different agencies. In addition to the pressure resulting from the committee's routine operation and from the placement efforts of the Democratic party and the White House staff, there were other influences on government agencies, particularly those in the public eye. The very structure of the Equal Employment Opportunity Committee afforded the occasion and reinforcement for such influence. The presence on the committee, for example, of John Macy, chairman of the Civil Service Commission, helped not only in integrating committee activities with those of the commission, but also in allowing the commission to exert informal pressure. For instance, Macy called the attention of the Secretary of Health, Education, and Welfare (at the time, Anthony Celebrezze) to a pattern suggesting discrimination in the Social Security Administration during the first year of the equal employment program. Since Celebrezze was also a member of the committee it was a friendly exchange for informational purposes that led to immediate corrective measures without any formal action on the record at all.

From the beginning the committee's action was aimed at securing positive action and setting up machinery within the various agencies that would take over much of the responsibility for implementation of the program. As was evident as early as Roosevelt's wartime fair employment program, no

---

[18] Joseph Kraft, "Washington Insight," *Harper's*, June 1964, p. 112.

[19] Harold Fleming, "The Federal Executive and Civil Rights," *Daedulus*, Fall 1965, p. 926.

small organization could police the entire federal establishment. The solution that had been adopted beginning with Eisenhower was the designating within each agency of a deputy employment officer whose function it was to secure, interpret, and adjudge compliance with the equal employment order in his agency. The deputy {39} employment officer was part father confessor, part poster of billboard announcements, part judge, part transmitter of complaints. The function was ill-defined and remains ill-defined to this day. In some agencies the equal employment program is carried out in a separately established division with active participation in recruitment, enforcement, and hearings. In others, it has been merely a formal paper allocation of a responsibility never or seldom exercised.

The handling of individual complaints was regarded as secondary to the committee's over-all responsibility for establishing positive machinery to deal with the problem of discrimination. Complaints, although seriously considered and even elaborately and lavishly documented in some instances, were regarded by the committee as more important as symptoms than for their own sake; a complaint was regarded as indicating where problems had developed in an agency and was to be used as an opening wedge for inquiry into the total picture of the agency's disposition of problems.

IV

With the strong support the Committee on Equal Employment Opportunity had in the White House during Kennedy's presidency, the committee's record was basically a good one. The growth of Negro employment was sustained throughout the federal service. Indeed the charge of "reverse discrimination" arose in subdued but definite fashion and even received some documentary support. The success of the equal employment opportunity program was undoubtedly due to the efforts of all concerned, hardly to the efforts of the committee alone, which never became noted for aggressiveness of tactics or efficiency. Nevertheless, its record was rather more impressive than that of any previous such establishment.

The committee reported that to November 1963 it had processed 2,243 cases, of 2,699 complaints made, with 36 percent resulting in "corrective action" as compared with 16 percent for the Committee on Government Employment Policy and 23 percent for the wartime Committee on Fair Employment Practice.[20] (Its success with private industry was also notable—72 percent compared with about 20 percent for the President's Committee on Government Contracts.) These figures {40} are perhaps less significant than may appear at first glance since the committee's definition of "corrective action" was always rather generous, including any sort of promotion for the

---

[20] President's Committee on Equal Employment Opportunity, *Report to the President*, November 26, 1963, pp. 105-106.

individual or readjustment in his job whether or not instigated by the complaint or the committee findings. Corrective action, in short, might have been purely an artifact of, time; in many instances general re-evaluation of a position, which took place irrespective of the complaint of the jobholder, emerged as a favorable statistic in committee reports. In only rare instances did the committee formally find evidence of discrimination, its attitude being that the finding of discrimination was on the whole not a necessary part of its. operation. Administrators felt that the label needlessly aroused contention and that more positive results could be achieved by other means. Yet to Negro groups and critics of the committee, the formal finding of discrimination would in itself have been an indication of sincerity and a token of intent. The lack of such candor, the unwillingness to call names, in their eyes indicated doubt and hesitancy on the part of the committee. This difference in outlook was to persist.

The advent of President Johnson's administration did not result in any lessening in prominence of the program. On the contrary there were a series of emphatic statements of support by the President, who, after all, had been the chief architect of the committee's program during his term as Vice President, and energetic backing in action by the White House staff. However, some shift in style became evident with the growth in power on the committee of Hobart Taylor, who had been personally chosen for this post by Johnson. "Hobart is essentially a fixer," one of the more prominent civil rights leaders explained privately, His method was that of a private negotiator seeking to reach a solution for a specific incident, while the logic of the program required the development of broad machinery independent of specific situations. Taylor devoted his attention primarily to the committee's work on contract compliance, His division of time between the committee and his functions in the President's office, together with his approach to routine administration, seemed to be reflected in a general lack of tautness in the organization as a whole.

During the 1964 campaign the Democratic party stressed its achievement and its pledges in the field of equal employment, as against the record of a candidate labeled relatively indifferent if not hostile to civil rights. With Goldwater's vote against the Civil Rights Act of 1964 {41} as an ever-present point of contrast, President Johnson again and again made specific references to the intent of his administration to eliminate all signs of discrimination and indicated that "this administration is irrevocably committed" to the achievement of equal employment, not only in the federal service, but throughout the society. Certainly he made it clear that it was unconscionable to have discrimination in the public sector, though its manifestations were to be rooted out everywhere, The choice of Hubert Humphrey, the liberal senator from Minnesota, as vice presidential candidate betokened the same commitment.

President Johnson's representatives on the Democratic National Committee were instrumental in issuing campaign material aimed at the Negro vote—including one pamphlet which listed by name and title the major Negro appointments of the past few years. The party also issued a release (November 23, 1964) summarizing the gains achieved by Negroes in elective offices, concluding that there were 250 Negroes in elective positions in 33 states, all but 10 of whom were Democrats. (The release also gave names, addresses, and phone numbers of such Negroes, presumably for organizational purposes.) The intent of the administration to secure further Negro gains was evidenced by the subsequent choice of Thurgood Marshall as Solicitor General of the United States and other appointments at various levels of high and middling positions throughout the government.

The newly elected Vice President Humphrey was named chairman of the Committee on Equal Employment Opportunity, as Lyndon Johnson had been before him. Apparently, however, Hobart Taylor's influence had already become pervasive with the committee. In any event, the general tenor of operation of the administrative staff was clearly fixed. The Vice President was apparently not too happy with this arrangement and sought some changes. He was probably influenced by the fact that by late 1964 the civil rights picture had altered and there was now a plethora of organizations in the field. Responsibilities in this field were exercised by the Community Relations Service and such departments as Labor, as well as the President's committee. Most important was the Equal Employment Opportunity Commission, created by Title VII of the Civil Rights Act of 1964. It was given power to prevent discrimination in private employment directly, not merely through government contract provisions. The notion of a superimposed coordinating staff was strongly pressed by the Department of Justice, {42} and the Vice President accepted that recommendation. On February 7, 1985, the White House made public a letter to the Vice President dated February 5, indicating the President's agreement with Humphrey's "recommendation that there be a comparatively simple coordinating mechanism without elaborate staff and organization." Executive Order 11197 which accompanied the letter established the President's Council on Equal Opportunity with the Vice President as chairman, and with representation from no fewer than seventeen agencies actively concerned with civil rights.

The problems of coordination were not small. The Civil Rights Act of 1964 itself presented several problems of interpretation and allocations of responsibility. Section 701b provided "that it shall be the policy of the United States to ensure equal employment opportunity for federal employees without discrimination because of race, color, religion, sex, or national origin, and the President shall utilize his existing authority to effectuate this policy." (This provision was inserted in lieu of a rather broad one suggested by Senator Everett Dirksen of Illinois which would have explicitly prohibited discrimination in public employment generally.[21] Such a provision would have meant

---

[21] Donald King and Charles Quick, *Legal Aspects of the Civil Rights Movement* (Detroit: Wayne State University Press, 1965), pp. 316-317.

not only legislative outlawing of federal discrimination, but assumption by the federal government of direct authority to deal with state and local discrimination as well—a proposal which was to draw support in 1965 but which in 1964 was still seen as premature. The major impetus for enacting this kind of legislation appears to have come from southerners unfriendly to the equal employment program, perhaps with the thought of complicating the program, or more likely with the thought of preventing the passage of the legislation in its entirety.) While Section 709d specifically exempted those already reporting to the President's committee under Executive Order 10925 from the provisions of the bill, it did not provide a clear-cut line of division between the President's committee and the newly created Equal Employment Opportunity Commission.

Nonetheless, the act constituted the first congressional mention of the President's Committee on Equal Employment Opportunity and the executive order, and seemingly gave the program legitimacy, falsely suggesting congressional acceptance of the program. In spring 1984, however, Senator Willis Robertson (Democrat of Virginia) of the Appropriations {43} Committee found an effective weapon against the President's committee, described well by Christopher Pyle and Richard Morgan,[22] The inter-agency aspect of the President's committee had enabled it to operate through existing budgets without having to defend its operations to Congress and account closely for its costs. "Since the program's expenditures were split and buried in the appropriation bills of 18 participating departments and agencies (often under such titles as 'procurement,' contract administration,' and 'a study of equal employment opportunity') the Committee was able to channel well over $3 million into the investigative effort. Close to $1 million was also spent annually by the President's Committee itself out of contributions supplied directly by participating agencies.... In contrast the new [Equal Employment Opportunity] Commission fought a battle-royal for its funds this summer before the committees of Congress and came out with only $2.7 million, much of which will have to be spent on costly complaint investigations."[23] Robertson's tactic was to cut from the appropriations bill of each contributing agency a sum equal to its contribution to the committee's expenses. "The cuts were later explained as protests against the excessive use of this indirect method of financing by the Executive branch generally, but a check of the budgets of similar units, such as the Committee on Physical Fitness and the Committee on Employing the Handicapped, shows that the attack was pressed only against the civil rights unit.[24]

---

[22] "Johnson's Civil Rights Shake-Up," *New Leader*, October 11, 1965, pp. 3-7.

[23] *Ibid.*, p. 4.

[24] *Ibid.* It is perhaps not irrelevant to note that not until April 1965 was a Negro page ever hired to serve congressmen. See *New York Times*, April 14, 1965, p. 24.

The Vice President saw the difficulties involved in requiring the agencies to contribute to the financing of the work of the President's committee when the amounts needed had been cut from their budgets, and he arranged a three-month moratorium with the Appropriations Committee, promising by September 30 either to phase out the President's committee or to seek a direct appropriation for its support from Congress. The determining considerations in the final disposition of the matter are shrouded in the normal mysteries of politics. It is generally agreed that Humphrey, after looking over the situation, decided that the federal program would best be turned over to the Civil Service Commission. However, Pyle and Morgan suggest that it was his intention {44} virtually to the eve of the deadline merely to abolish the President's committee and transfer the contract compliance functions to the President's Council on Equal Opportunity, even though the latter was intended only as a coordinating and not an operating unit.[25] In any event, the Vice President in a letter dated September 24, 1965, recommended to the President the abolition of both the President's Committee on Equal Employment Opportunity and the President's Council on Equal Opportunity and the movement of all their functions into regular departments and the Civil Service Commission. Perhaps his decision to, in effect, withdraw personally was an acknowledgment that the tactics that had proved successful in dealing with the President's committee could also be used against the Council on Equal Employment; more likely it was a result of sheer political pressures and some loss of power by Humphrey.

Pyle and Morgan suggest that this represented a stunning loss of face for the Vice President—he lost two of his major titles—and a setback for the civil rights movement as well. A letter of explanation by the Vice President to the *New Leader* on November 8, 1965,[26] does not dispel the impression that Pyle and Morgan were correct in their analysis, although in this letter and in an earlier press conference the Vice President logically and coherently indicated that he based his major recommendations upon the need to "keep people from getting in each other's way" in dealing with the civil rights question broadly conceived.[27] Some of the arrangements suggest a desire for less zeal and more legalism in dealing with the programs.

The withdrawal of Vice President Humphrey from official connection with the program was viewed with dismay by civil rights organizations gener-

---

[25] *Ibid.*

[26] Letter to the editor, *New Leader*, November 8, 1965, p. 33.

[27] On the day of the Vice President's letter to the President, Humphrey held a press conference to announce his recommendation. Presidential press secretary Bill Moyers, Attorney General Katzenbach, and Secretary of Labor Wirtz were also present. (Hobart Taylor had a short time earlier been appointed to the Export-Import Bank and therefore was no longer involved in the committee's activities.) White House Press Conference Mimeograph No. 119A.

ally, and the transfer of the Community Relations Service from the Department of Commerce into the Department of Justice was opposed openly by civil rights leaders. The later resignation of the acting director of the service in opposition to the reorganization and his replacement by the nephew of Roy Wilkins of course had some effect {45} in mitigating this hostility.[28] The most important single development, however, was the transfer of the contract compliance division of the President's committee into the Department of Labor, notoriously a weak department and one with little logical relation to the function it was assigned. Secretary of Labor Wirtz's lack of political leverage, dramatically revealed when he was unable to fire his own undersecretary because of the objections of AFL-CIO head George Meany, added to the implausibility of his being able to be militant in this realm.

In contrast, determination that the "in-house" program of the President's committee should be transferred to the Civil Service Commission was apparently an easy and relatively noncontroversial matter. The Civil Service Commission was credited by Pyle and Morgan with being "apparently eager to set up a tough new program to promote equal opportunity within the federal establishment."[29] Though the *New Leader* writers were skeptical of the Civil Service Commission's ability to pursue the program effectively, there were undoubted advantages in the transfer to the commission, including the possibility of minimizing duplication of channels and establishing more orderly procedures. What was lost was, of course, the advantage of a second structure, for the Civil Service Commission had always had a program of its own, even during the existence of the President's committee.

In ultimate terms, the restoration of the "in-house" program to the Civil Service Commission was inevitable. It is a personnel function which ought to be exercised in the normal civil service manner. The function was of course taken from the Civil Service Commission precisely to dramatize, distinguish, and symbolize the uniqueness of the program, to indicate priorities, and to demonstrate lack of confidence in the commission's zeal in promoting civil rights. The question now is whether the timing was appropriate, whether the program had achieved a sufficient level of maturity in the federal service generally. Only time will tell whether the recent actions of Congress have prematurely or at the appropriate time forced the remerger of these personnel functions.

---

[28] *New York Times*, December 15, 1965, p. 24.

[29] *New Leader*, October 11, 1965, p. 5.

3
Representative Bureaucracy and Civil Rights

I

{46}
THE cruciality of bureaucracy and bureaucratic representation to any rising minority group—indeed to any group interested in social power is but thinly veiled and seldom truly hidden. The paradox of bureaucratic power is well encapsulated in the title of a book by Eric Strauss, *The Ruling Servants*.[1] The formal employee relationship of the bureaucrat to the general public is not entirely a myth; yet the mysteries of regulations and the advantages of expertise all too often mean that power flows the other way. It is rare that either the public or the civil servant sees the bureaucrat as in fact subservient.

The same ambiguity prevails concerning all public officeholding. On the one hand we hold that public service is a privilege, and thus we emphasize its desirability. On the other hand we speak of public office as a burden, of an officeholder making a sacrifice—a concept advocated particularly by officeholders themselves or aspirants to office. Office seekers often act out a milder form of the inaugural of the medieval bishop the dragging to the altar of a nominally reluctant candidate who must proclaim "Nolo episcopari," "I don't want to be bishop."

The question of whether officeholding is a privilege or a burden immediately raises another question—who shall have access to positions {47} of governmental authority. Strangely, to our view, social class, family, and other particularistic claims have had more support than sheer merit as bases for selection of officeholders.

Through history restriction of the opportunity to hold public office has been an effective instrument of social control. Indeed patterns of restricted access to the public service have been utilized by scholars as useful and revealing indices of distribution and concentration of social power.[2] Conversely, the expansion of officeholding opportunities is usually an indication

---

[1] Eric Strauss, *The Ruling Servants* (New York: Praeger, 1961).

[2] See, for example, Harold Lasswell, Daniel Lerner, and C. E. Rothwell, *The Comparative Study of Elites* (Stanford, Calif.: Hoover Institute, Stanford University Press, 1952), and Suzanne Keller, *Beyond the Ruling Class* (New York: Random House, 1963), especially Chapter 3.

of the general opening up of opportunities in a society.³

The American War of Independence cry "No taxation without representation" in all probability reflected mostly a desire for no taxation at all. Yet it also reflected, at this early period, an understanding of the connection between type of government personnel and policy outcomes. The Jacksonian revolt—widely proclaimed a spoils raid was in fact based on the assumption that greater rotation of officeholders was desirable and that there was to be no vested interest in office. Even in a stable society such as that of the United States, social groups have been adroit and at times aggressive in claiming their right to serve in high positions as well as low. Historians have paid particular attention to the changing tide of officeholders, and have not failed to note the significance of the voicing of new claims and the advent of new groups to public office.

Recent Negro efforts to attain greater access to the government service have, then, parallels in past aspirations and achievements of other groups. But the demand of Negroes for a representative share in the bureaucracy reflects a fairly new concept.

Representation in the sense of personification is of course an old idea in political theory. The symbolization or embodiment of the community in the person of the leader, who in turn responsively and conscientiously represents community values, is basic to most political thought of {48} ancient and medieval times, as well as that of the modern era. But the concepts of cross-sectional representativeness and a more or less democratic choice of representatives are both, with a few exceptions, largely post-medieval phenomena.⁴ The rather unusual procedures for selection of officials utilized by Athens in the fifth century B.C. much like those in a lottery suggest democracy to some modern observers. Generally, though, the first truly modern note on representation is sounded in the writings of Marsilius of Padua and William of Occam, precursors of modern attitudes in this, as in much else. The idea that representatives must be drawn from all elements of society is in any refined sense largely a product of the eighteenth and nineteenth centuries; it was almost unprecedented when asserted by the American colonies. (Actually, this claim was not fully acknowledged in England at least until the reform bills of the nineteenth century.) Indeed, the view that a body of selected representatives should be a microcosmic reproduction of the social and political cleavages in the community is almost, strictly speaking, contemporaneous. By and large, even the great legislative bodies of Western democracy have been a

---

³ See, for example, in the work of Robert Brown the discussion of American Revolutionary society and in the work of L. B. Namier and disciples the discussion of British parliaments. Karl A. Wittfogel has suggested a simpler index of social power—the relative postures required of subjects toward rulers—in *Oriental Despotism* (New Haven, Conn.: Yale University Press, 1957), especially pp. 152-154.

⁴ Francis Coker and Carlton Rodee, "Representation," *Encyclopedia of the Social Sciences*.

hybrid of elite representation, the best leadership of the community, and representation of the community as a whole.[5]

The application to the bureaucracy of any notion of representativeness seems to have been an exclusive development of the past thirty years or so. J. Donald Kingsley is generally credited with having coined the term "representative bureaucracy" when he utilized that phrase as the title of a book less than a quarter of a century ago. Perhaps even more striking is the fact, borne out in a study of the literature, that to a large extent it was Kingsley who articulated the concept for the first time in an even halfway systematic form.[6]

This late development is hardly surprising. Not only did there have to be acceptance of the idea of representativeness in relation to elective officials before transference of the idea by analogy to other public officials; but there also bad to be recognition of the function and importance of the bureaucracy itself before much attention would be given {49} to its composition. This recognition came in large part only after the work of Max Weber focused attention on bureaucratic structures and after the civil service had become regularized and stabilized by the adoption of a merit system. Any discussion of representative bureaucracy as it is related to the quest for equal opportunity must first take into account these developments.

II

Weber suggests that the modern bureaucracy was developed by the prince as he tried to centralize authority in his own hands, taking it away from the dispersed gentry.[7] Feudalism in its primary form consisted of the carrying out of public duties by decentralized vassals who derived satisfactions and maintenance from local financial privileges and who functioned in their public capacities without obvious public support. An initial step away from such dispersal was the establishment of dependency of public officials upon what Weber calls "prebendaries," i.e., economic prerogatives held at the pleasure of the prince. While the officeholding gentry still normally maintained their power without direct salary from the public treasury, they usually were given some indirect economic advantage as a consequence of their political power. When economic advantage became attached to political power in an overt way, the gentry normally were more clearly at the mercy of the prince. The weakness of the "prebendary system" was that with local funds still basically supplying the economic needs of this cryptobureaucrat,

---

[5] C. K. Allen, *Democracy and the Individual* (New York: Oxford University Press, 1943), pp. 21-22.

[6] J. Donald Kingsley, *Representative Bureaucracy* (Yellow Springs, Ohio: Antioch Press, 1944).

[7] H. H. Gerth and C. W. Mills, editors, *From Max Weber* (New York: Oxford University Press, 1958), pp. 80-83.

his loyalties tended to be locally oriented as well. In order to establish unequivocally the fact that maintenance was at the pleasure of the prince, there was a need to centralize the means of payment to officials.

Thus, as Weber points out, the transference of authority to a central government is accompanied by a rise in the budget of the public treasury, for the transfer substituted salaried officials for those who formerly performed the function without overt payment. "The whole process is a complete parallel to the development of the capitalist enterprise through gradual expropriation of the independent producers."[8] In effecting this centralization the prince drew upon previously unutilized {50} talent in the society to undercut the gentry and their authority. The new officeholders were generally persons with uncertain status, who lacked strong social and institutional support—the clergy, the literati, and lawyers. The lack of a secure footing in society by an aspirant to an office was viewed as a positive advantage by a manipulating centralizer, far such a person would not have the mass support that might enable him to translate his position into an independent basis for his own authority. (Wittfogel, following Weber, notes that eunuchs are the extreme case in the use of such free-floating talent.[9])

Weber further suggests that since the prince essentially was attempting to create new standards and to destroy old bases for distribution of power, he also tended to stress universalistic claims. These were useful in centralizing authority in order to supplant particularistic claims based on family or tribal lines. His purpose, however, was augmentation of his own power. Following this argument, Wittfogel has suggested that the development in Imperial China of "objective" tests for civil service in fact enlarged the power of the emperor without appreciably opening up public careers to those with talent. While some contest the actual historical result, it is conceded by scholars that the primary purpose was enlargement of the emperor's control.[10]

In an effort to preserve their own authority, the bureaucrats assembled under the control of the prince eventually rationalized their own assumption of independent status by either claiming a higher loyalty e.g., to the regime— or appealing to some familialistic notions of right to office. In a democracy, the bureaucracy, for example, argues that some definitive authority should be vested in itself as a check on the chief executive so that the concentration of absolute power is prevented and a democratic order maintained.

Of all such claims that of loyalty to the community, and its organized component, the regime, has probably been the most significant. In the Western world the notion of a neutral public service—one loyal not merely to the

---

[8] *Ibid.*, p. 82.

[9] Wittfogel, *Oriental Despotism*, pp. 847ff.

[10] See the selections assembled by Johanna M. Menzel, *The Chinese Civil Service: Career Open to Talent?* (Boston: Heath, 1968).

particular officeholder but to any legitimate successor—is sometimes traced to the development of the London police force. Where such bureaucracies are effectively centralized, loyalty and responsibility are owed not just to the particular officeholder or even to {51} the more generalized policies of a person or government but to a regime, perduring beyond the lifetime of any individual officeholder.[11] The advent of democracy greatly encourages such loyalty to a regime, for its processes emphasize the possibility of peaceable and ordered succession in governmental authority; it in short institutionalizes turnover.

But a paradox arises. If loyalty to an established order is sought, then the desideratum might well be the social distribution of officeholding on localized and familialistic grounds rather than concentration in the hands of a single group. Such a distribution affords many hostages to stability; the incorporation of representatives of different social groups into the enforcement machinery involves these groups with the policy itself and commits them to its maintenance. Participation, even if only in the implementation of policy on the part of lower-rung officeholders, makes less salient and less risky the role of top officeholders. Lower-rung officeholders feel some commitment to a policy over which they have a measure of control and transmit that sense of responsibility to the groups in which they are socially anchored. Additionally—perhaps more accurately, supplementarily—such a social distribution eases the problem of securing compliance. Access to representatives of a broad spectrum of social forces has at many times been a means by which ruling groups have secured obedience. In its crudest form such access might involve the taking of personal hostages or the inclusion of women of differing nationalities, races, and religions in the king's harem. Indeed informal consultative session was the rudimentary nucleus of the parliament, which brought together men from different parts of the nation so that they could be given information about new policies of the king; they then were expected to go back to their communities and secure adherence to these policies, which all too often involved the collection of new taxes.

While bureaucracies could claim independent status under any conditions, they were most likely to achieve it in situations where they were both significant in numbers and reasonably powerful. On the whole the prince was reluctant to grant such independence where there was no need to concede it. The assertion of a loyalty that transcends the person of the ruler is in fact therefore usually also a rudimentary {52} assertion of the expertise and authority of the bureaucracy.[12] Hitler's requirement of an oath of loyalty to his

---

[11] David Easton and Robert Hess, "Youth and the Political System," in S. M. Lipset and Leo Lowenthal, editors, *Culture and Social Character* (New York: Free Press, 1961), pp. 226-252.

[12] S. N. Eisenstadt, *The Political Systems of Empires* (New York: Free Press, 1983), Chapter 8, especially p. 159.

person from all bureaucrats was consequently clearly a throwback, a reversal of the normal development of bureaucracy.[13] The modern rational democratic state has usually gone hand in hand with a bureaucratic governmental structure.

It was Weber who, to a large extent, formulated this development and delineated it. Sometimes credit is claimed for Saint-Simon. But this on the whole is a misunderstanding of the writings of that interesting and perverse man. Indeed Saint-Simon can be regarded as primarily a critic of the bureaucracy and a devotee of quite a different class of experts, the technocrats. He has become known as the advocate of the managerial autocracy, but his concept of the manager was largely that of a physical and scientific expert rather than a specialist in human relationships and the structured flow of events. His attitude toward bureaucracy was rather like that of Lenin who believed that with wider dissemination of arithmetic all men could manage factories. In his celebrated suggestion that France would be paralyzed by the loss of fifty of her best physicists and chemists but would be just as well off without "Monsieur the King's brother," Saint-Simon included the bureaucrats and lesser officials as ones whose loss would be lamentable from the standpoint of humanity and ethics but who would be easy to replace from the standpoint of efficiency. The valuable people are "the scientists, artists and artisans, the only men whose work is a positive utility to society and cost it practically nothing, who are kept down by the princes and other rulers, who are simply more or less incapable bureaucrats." The dross of society, includes, for Saint-Simon, "the governing class from the Prime Minister to the humblest clerk."[14]

The same lumping together of "rulers"—whether legislative or executive—with the typical bureaucrat is to be found in the discussions of Mosca, Pareto, and Michels.[15] While these writers advance our appreciation of the general significance of functionaries and elites they {53} do so in terms of a broad societal model that does not differentiate between the various organs of government.

Weber, of course, did recognize the special attributes of bureaucracy and bureaucrats. But at times even he discussed the bureaucrat in the same general framework as the political leader, without acknowledgment of their separate status. Thus in his discussion of "Politics as a Vocation" the political executive tends to merge with the civil servant, perhaps appropriately in that context. But his general emphasis upon the quite distinct career lines of the

---

[13] Frederic Burin, "Bureaucracy and National Socialism," in R. K. Merton *at al.*, *Reader in Bureaucracy* (Glencoe, Ill.: Free Press, 1947), pp. 38-47.

[14] F. M. H. Markham, editor, *Henri Comte de Saint-Simon: Selected Writings* (New York: Macmillan, 1952), pp. 74, 78.

[15] For a recent and thoughtful introduction to this school of thought, see Keller, *Beyond the Ruling Class*.

two sorts of functionaries clarified the limitations of the civil servantry. Thus he avoided such fallacious predictions of the control of modern society by bureaucrats as that of James Burnham, who insisted that the civil servant was controlling Nazi Germany at a time when in fact the civil service was at the nadir of power and influence.[16] As Weber explicitly recognized, the typical bureaucrat is a socially exploitable climber with little independent social power. Indeed, as Weber only partially recognized, expertise, though buttressed by the trappings of the aristocracy, may not prevail against a dedicated and relentless executive determined to effect control in policy, even at the cost of efficiency,[17] In all bureaucracies, the modal personality who is rewarded for his activity is the "can-do bureaucrat"—on the order of Ralph Turner's "can-do" bursar[18]—is who manages to find a means to meet the bills incurred by his superiors, rather than the stickler who tries to pursue formal organizational goals. It is after all the bureaucrats and the managers who have generally committed Benda's crime of *The Treason at Clerks* and have been subservient to top policy makers, whether these latter base their power upon political or economic means. But before there was a need to stress the weakness of the bureaucrat, it was first necessary to recognize his importance. This Weber emphatically did.

The perception of the importance of the bureaucracy has of course stimulated unrepresented groups to seek access to it in order to gain influence. The standard of equitable universalistic recruitment also increases pressures. Where there are in theory no barriers, the actual denial of representation in public service becomes even more obviously {54} an affront to dispossessed groups. Such a denial becomes a crude challenge to the loyalty, worth, and power of an unrepresented social group. Consciousness of the growth in size and significance of bureaucracy, emphasis of theorists upon its importance, and even the perception of its relevance as an index of social power all combine to encourage hitherto unheard-from social groups in their demands for appointive, as well as elective, positions in the public service.

III

In the United States and Great Britain, new attitudes toward government service came not so much as concomitants of a drive for egalitarianism but rather as a result of an effort to eradicate past abuses. Civil service reform was achieved under clearly moralistic slogans—perhaps to a shade greater extent in the United States than in Britain in which efficiency and economy were

---

[16] See James Burnham, *The Managerial Revolution* (New York: John Day, 1941).

[17] Burin, "Bureaucracy and National Socialism," in Merton *et al.*, *Reader in Bureaucracy*, pp. 33-41.

[18] Ralph Turner, "The Navy Disbursing Officer as a Bureaucrat," *American Sociological Review*, 12: 342-348 (June 1947).

advocated, not only as means to save the taxpayer money but also as standards for employment that were mete and just. Though the upper-middle-class reformers constituted a group which might have obtained a disproportionate return from particularistic standards, they saw that it was only proper for government to eliminate preference and applauded efficiency because it was right as much as because it was cheap—although the latter was not forgotten.[19]

A break with the past was clearly in order, In England the pleasant nepotism caricatured by Dickens was described in more scathing terms in the Northcote-Trevelyan report which called for drastic reform. The custom of utilizing government service as a place of refuge for upper-class incompetents with strong political connections (in Kingsley's terms the "eleemosynary concept of the State,"[20] in more recent parlance the concept of a "welfare state in reverse") seemed indefensible. The demand was that all who served the state should in fact earn their keep, even the upper classes!

Kingsley describes the old pattern of recruitment in the British civil {55} service in harsh terms. Following Robert Lowe, he suggests the essential truth of the latter's sweeping assertion that in the Old Regime "there was never such a thing known as a man being appointed to a clerkship in a public office because he was supposed to be fit for the place."[21] Perversely, many appointments were given to persons for reasons of ill health.

In the United States, party patronage and party loyalty were the abuses arousing the ire of reformers. The reformers had no roseate or universal scheme of positive equality in mind. They did not seek, for example, social quotas or representation for women—but they did know "what they didn't like." To this day the civil service mechanism is primarily a means for keeping undesirables out of office and undesirable criteria from being implemented. As critics of civil service from John Fischer to Walter Carpenter have pointed out, this does not guarantee that good men will necessarily be in office [22]

The lack of a true aristocratic class in the United States meant that government offices could not become sinecures of families. Nonetheless, a strong sense of property in office developed. Jefferson sought to introduce an element of representativeness into the bureaucracy, arguing, "is it political

---

[19] Paul Van Riper, *History of the United States Civil Service* (Evanston, Ill.: Row, Peterson, 1958), pp. 26-27, 184-185; Ari Hoogenboom, *Outlawing the Spoils* (Urbana: University of Illinois Press, 1961), especially p. 193. It is interesting to note that Garfield saw civil service and education as major solutions to the Negro problem. Eli Ginzberg and Alfred S. Eichner, *The Troublesome Presence: American Democracy and the Negro* (New York: Free Press, 1964). p. 235.

[20] Kingsley, *Representative Bureaucracy*, pp. 28-30.

[21] *Ibid.*, p. 35.

[22] John Fischer, "Let's Go Back to the Spoils System," *Harper's*, October 1945, pp. 362-368, and Walter Seal Carpenter, *The Unfinished Business of Civil Service Reform* (Princeton, NJ.: Princeton University Press, 1952).

intolerance to claim a proportionate share in the direction of the public affairs?" But in a reply in the *New York Evening Post* William Coleman probably with the assistance of Alexander Hamilton—indicated that such a policy was a violation of an "implicit contract," by which it was understood that those investing their time and efforts in public service might stay on and continue to reap the benefits of their previous service in conditions that would permit them, military veterans and others deserving of the public patrimony, to "spend the evening of [their] days in ease and competence.[23]

It was against the idea of a property right in public office that the Jacksonians revolted. They challenged the notion that once in office a person may retain such a position permanently. The counter-theory, which became conspicuous with Jackson, can clearly be traced to Jefferson, who emphasized the right of a political party in power to replace {56} incumbents on grounds other than dishonesty or inefficiency. Actually there is no evidence of a large-scale dismissal of officials under Jackson and the estimates of actual turnover indicate that perhaps 10 percent, and not more than 20 percent, were in fact displaced.[24]

American development, then, followed the path laid down by Weber. The existence of a bureaucracy devoted to regularized procedures engendered the demand that the bureaucracy itself be regularized in nature. Political privilege in appointment suggested the possibility of political privilege in the carrying out of the bureaucratic function; conversely, it was argued, regularized, efficient procedures in selection of officeholders, a "merit system," would lead to a better and more democratic civil service.

The opposition to the merit system proceeded on much the same line of reasoning, as would be necessary in a democratic society, but in defensive tones. It was suggested that the merit system and a career service would establish a privileged class. Entrenchment of career men in public office was seen as leading to the creation of an aristocracy. To counter this picture of an officed nobility, the advocates of the Pendleton Act had to invoke even more decisively antidemocratic symbols like the "boss" and the "machine."

But in none of this was there a conscious application of the principle of equality of opportunity in any social or economic sense. Indeed, this notion developed rather more slowly in the United States than in Great Britain. As early as 1914, the second Royal Commission on the Civil Service (1912-1914) specifically recommended equality of opportunity in the governmental service and suggested that there was a need for expansion of educational opportunity in order to achieve this. "The State as Employer and Examiner should co-

---

[23] Carl Russell Fish, *The Civil Service and the Patronage* (New York: Longmans Green, 1905), pp. 85-37.

[24] Van Riper, *History of the United States Civil Service*, pp. 159-160, relying on an investigation by Erik M. Eriksson, "The Federal Civil Service under President Jackson," *Mississippi Valley Historical Review*, 13:524 (March 1927).

operate more closely than it has apparently done hitherto with the State as Educator...."[25] The social divisions in Great Britain were so well established that calculated planning and statement of policy were necessary if reformers were to achieve any breakthrough at all.

In the United States the achievement of egalitarianism in the civil service was much more gradual, haphazard, and pragmatic. So women gradually won acceptance in the civil service—first as "female clerks" {57} who could be hired at a cheaper rate than men—later in other positions.[26] Since the enunciated principles of the merit system proclaimed the absence of discrimination, new policies were promulgated as purportedly supplemental, to enforce specifically what was already theoretically implicit in the general policy. But these regulations attracted little attention in promulgation and were subject to generally cursory treatment in effectuation. They were largely declaratory rather than efficacious. The previous exceptions to the general policy all too often perdured, although these discriminatory policies were now stamped as less legitimate than ever. Lacking the clarity of the new British policies, American reforms often evoked less response to the will of the enactor. But, paradoxically, changes in the American structure have come about more steadily, in accretive fashion; in Britain they have taken place only as the result of sharp policy shifts.

IV

Definition and discussion of "representative bureaucracy" is almost nonexistent, Kingsley contented himself with suggesting that administrative personnel should be drawn from all social classes, and gave little attention to any other consideration. Even a writer like James McCamy, author of several books and articles which at least in part hinge on the concept, has never made an explicit statement of any length on this subject. The most advanced formulation that I could find was in his textbook on American government, in a chapter under the heading "Representative Government: The Executive," where the following statement appears: "It is important for the attitudes of these permanent officials that they be selected to be representative of society."[27]

Presumably everyone regards it as axiomatic that representative bureaucracies like representative legislatures are good things and need no further defense; hence the lack of discussion. It can be suggested, however, that there are a number of discrete concepts of representative bureaucracy and separate

---

[25] Quoted in Kingsley, *Representative Bureaucracy*, p. 100.

[26] Van Riper, *History of the United States Civil Service*, p. 85.

[27] James L. McCamy, *American Government* (New York: Harper, 1957), p. 638. See also his *Conduct of the New Diplomacy* (New York: Harper and Row, 1964). But see Van Riper's *History of the United States Civil Service*, pp. 551ff.

justifications for it, and identification of these would seem worthwhile.

Representative bureaucracy may be sought in order to create a microcosm of the community. This concept suggests that the bureaucracy, {58} like the legislature, should be a funnel for divergent points of view and fails if it does not have this Gallup Poll-like quality. Such representativeness has the advantage—already mentioned in this chapter—that social responsibility is thereby shared and diffused, which can lead to general acceptance of governmental programs and policies. Wide distribution of the members of the bureaucracy also operates to secure compliance, since they presumably urge support through broad sectors of the population. A representative bureaucracy, it has also been claimed, is more likely than a bureaucracy dependent on a single class to have employees with diverse skills and talents and with the imagination necessary to deal with problems that emerge; for example, it has been suggested that a representative foreign service is more likely than a monolithic group to apprehend strange points of view in a foreign country.[28] Then too the diffusion of social responsibility not only legitimizes individual policies in the regime generally, but also brings to the representative members of all segments of the society who occupy public positions a broader social point of view than they would otherwise have had; they in turn transmit this socialization experience to others in their social groups.[29] Finally, we may note that a group supports a regime and identifies with it insofar as it has a stake in the system. Such a stake may involve policy considerations but it also involves the group's sharing of honorific status and of societal jobs generally with other groups in the society. Since governmental employment constitutes a larger proportion of the total economy in more complex societies, and since the function of leading the community is a highly valued one, such sharing is an expected concomitant of a democratic—usually technically advanced—society. The degree of such sharing is a good index of concentration of social power and its absence may signal lack of identification with the regime on the part of deprived groups.

Societies only imperfectly achieve this diffusion in their bureaucracies; sometimes unrepresentativeness is by design, sometimes it results from unconscious development. Probably a perfectly representative bureaucracy is unachievable, for it would require uniform distribution of ability throughout the population and uniform interest in government service as well. Furthermore, governmental needs are not in exact {59} proportion to societal needs; the range of talents government demands is narrower than that required for society as a whole. Probably the composition of a governmental structure will always be predominantly clerical and middle class, Kingsley was the first to

---

[28] Richard Johnson, "The Representativeness of the American Foreign Service Officers Corps" (State Department report, undated, mimeographed), pp. 4-5.

[29] Samuel A. Stouffer, *Communism, Conformity and Civil Liberties* (New York: Doubleday, 1955).

criticize bureaucracies for their imperfect representativeness, their middle-class predominance. But the very nature of administration, and the technical requirements of organization, are likely to aggravate this type of disproportionate representation. Other types of inequitable recruitment to the public service—along religious, ethnic, caste, and linguistic lines—probably cause more difficulties in the world and are more readily subject to amelioration. Of course insofar as cleavages by religion or language or ethnic background parallel class lines or reinforce each other, they tend to become less manageable. Unfortunately, in most societies, such cleavages do tend to be mutually reinforcing and self-perpetuating, so that the Negro dilemma is in fact not unique but is rather re-enacted with variations throughout the world.

In Western European countries, the main deviations from representative bureaucracy are in the distribution of employees by social class and, secondarily, though quite significantly, by religion. As Chapman notes: "The scanty material available suggests that the majority of officials recruited in each class of the public service came from their corresponding social class and that the remainder come from the social class immediately below. This is of course what would reasonably be expected.... Social class in the public service does not work in reverse. The sons of members of the administrative class are to all intents and purposes never found lower down the scale. Unless they can join at their fathers' level they diverge into another profession."[30] The industrial working class and agricultural farm laborers are underrepresented throughout Western Europe. For example, only 10 percent of the Swedish higher officials came from the working class after twenty years of Social Democratic government. Probably parental opposition to education accounts for agricultural underrepresentation in France, Switzerland, Holland, and Denmark. Sometimes occupational and ethnic lines coincide as with the largely agricultural German-speaking population of South Tyrol.[31]

{60} Religion has been a ground for allocation of positions even in the United States. In New York City until very recently the presidencies of the city colleges were by convention allocated along religious lines. But it has been a more important criterion for employment in Europe. In Holland, the Catholic party was traditionally assigned the Ministry of Education and its "colonization," as Chapman calls it, was so successful that a Socialist Prime Minister refused to take over the ministry on the ground that he would be unable to work with the bulk of the bureaucrats there. Similarly the Ministry of the Middle Class in Belgium, the Ministry of Population in France, as well as specific ministries in other countries, have been regarded as Catholic preserves. Control of the Bavarian State Radio has likewise been restricted to

---

[30] Brian Chapman, *The Profession of Government* (London: Allen and Unwin, 1959), pp. 315-316.

[31] *Ibid.*, pp. 315-317.

Catholics. On the other hand, free thinkers and Free Masons often have gained control of some agencies. In France active participation in Free Masonry is still highly useful for anyone desiring advancement in some branches of the Ministry of the Interior.[32]

A special problem exists where duality of cultural and ethnic lines leads to bilingualism within the society, as in Canada or Belgium. "French-speaking Canadians have insistently brought up another problem—their role in the Federal Civil Service, where the dominant working language is English... 'I want my language to be respected in public places, particularly in federal offices' ... Some English-speaking Canadians both recognized and regretted this situation. Some even suggested changes, but the mere thought of bilingualism being officially imposed at this level seemed to cause a feeling of apprehension. Thus in Edmonton a civil servant stated—although in a perfectly cordial tone of voice, that 'if you require me after 17 years of service in the Civil Service, to pass and write an examination, to speak French, simply to keep my job, I'm afraid I will have to emigrate to Australia.'"[33]

In Israel where the population has a multi-cultural and multi-ethnic background, there is now general agreement that Hebrew is to be the spoken language, thus reducing tension on what had been a major issue. But a serious problem remains, for the style of thought, type of culture, and manner of decision-taking of Sephardim apparently constitute {61} a barrier similar to the ones the French-Canadians and the Belgian Flemish feel bar them from equal opportunity in their countries. The end result is the same in all three instances: the people of one ethnic-cultural background practically monopolize the upper reaches of the bureaucracy.

Many solutions to the problem of achieving a representative bureaucracy have been attempted by different societies. The most common is requirement of equitable geographic distribution. This may be effected by informal understanding as in the United States where federal judges, Cabinet officers, and the like are chosen in part to satisfy regional representation—or by specific provision as in Article 101 of the United Nations Charter, which states that "Due regard shall be paid to the importance of recruiting the staff on as wide a geographical basis as possible." For various reasons geographical distribution is generally accepted without controversy as providing a broad-gauge basis for selection of representatives. Due regard to geography very often will also give representation to racial and linguistic elements, and thus contribute to stability.

Another type of solution has been attempted in Lebanon where there is an allocation of political power generally on the basis of the presumed reli-

---

[32] *Ibid.*, pp. 284-286.

[33] *A Preliminary Report of the Royal Commission on Bilingualism and Biculturalism* (Ottawa: Queen's Printer, 1967), pp. 73-74.

gious distribution of the population. The result has been a limited stability. Since a new distribution based on the changing population lines might upset this stability, there has been no religious census since agreement was reached.[34]

In India there are constitutional quotas, based largely on population, for representation of the "untouchable" caste in both the national service and the local parliaments. Within the limits of the quotas untouchables qualify for positions in terms of their abilities. While the legislative seats are in practice now so apportioned and occupied, the allotment of civil service posts has not worked out quite so simply. Untouchables have qualified for lower-grade positions in greater numbers than there are positions as allocated by their proportion of the population, and they have been distinctly underrepresented in upper-class jobs. There were qualified candidates to fill only 1.3 percent of Class I governmental posts in 963, although the quota was 12.5 percent; less than {62} half of the allocated positions were filled in Classes II and 111.[35] The constitution of the former Malayan Federation provided for a more flexible arrangement, requiring establishment of reasonable quotas "to safeguard the special position of the Malays" in government service, education, and even business.[36] The government of Israel has deliberately solicited Sephardim for many governmental agencies, with a special effort in recent years being made in the Foreign Office. The Post Office and Police departments have by tradition had Sephardi ministers.

Preference to minority groups in access to educational facilities may be either a supplement to or a substitute for governmental employment quotas. In Great Britain bureaucratic reform was possible because of parallel changes in the public school system. Following the example set by the East India Company's school—Haileybury—the public schools made a place for the talented though impecunious. "The public schools merely effected a balance between rationalized organization and traditional power. In fact, the balance represented a compromise—between the reward of intellectual merit, on the one hand, and the reward of hereditary privilege, on the other."[37] In the old Malayan Federation, ethnic quotas for admission to a university were consciously employed in an attempt to avert predominance of the Chinese in the bureaucracy.

---

[34] Philip K. Hitti, *A Short History of Lebanon* (New York: St. Martin's Press, 1965), pp. 220-221.

[35] See M. N. Srinivas and André Béteille, "The 'Untouchables' of India," *Scientific American*, December 1965, pp. 13-17.

[36] Constitution, Federation of Malaya, Articles 40 and 153.

[37] Rupert Wilkinson, *Gentlemanly Power* (New York: Oxford University Press, 1964), pp. 22-23 and 10-11.

V

In contrast, the American effort to achieve a representative bureaucracy has been more volunteeristic, less rigid in prescribing goals, The American setup constitutes on the whole a novel experiment through emphasis on individual creative action.

This pattern in governmental service provides cues for the Negro youngster who must decide what educational course to pursue. It is difficult for a social group to change its traditional educational and occupational aspirations. Catholics have in recent years engaged in long discussions on the lack of an intellectual tradition in the American church and have concluded its absence is probably traceable to the fact that the Irish and Sicilians who form the backbone of Catholicism {63} in the United States have never emphasized intellectual values.[38] The record of the Jewish community in the United States in overcoming discrimination is often fallaciously contrasted with Negro achievement, overlooking the simple fact that the urban-intellectual values of contemporary Jewry comport well with the current needs of American society, while the values of the Negro community do not. On the other hand, efforts in Israel to change those Jewish social patterns in order to establish a strong agricultural base for the Israeli community have been only mildly successful in spite of tremendous ideological emphasis upon and financial support to that sector of the economy. The social inertia involved in occupational choice can be observed in walking or riding through the streets of any major city in the United States and noting the names on store fronts.

It is not easy for a Negro to seek out the type of training that is currently desired and needed in American society. Visible signs that such efforts will be rewarded are necessary. The Negro press has reported that Negroes still hesitate to go into engineering, where the demand for personnel is high, because they do not believe that they will, at the appropriate juncture in their careers, be regarded as promotable to supervisory positions. They prefer the "free-floating" professions of lawyer, teacher, doctor, and clergyman, in which they seldom face a "promotion" situation; or they go into agencies that have already demonstrated their willingness to make such promotions, i.e., government and welfare organizations.[39] The image of employment in large-scale organizations held by Negroes tends to be fairly accurate, though there is a time lag. Governmental service has always been seen as an attractive employment situation for the Negro, and yet it has also been believed by the Negro community that promotion within it is limited. By giving tangible

---

[38] The discussion begun by Monsignor John Tracy Ellis in 1955 was continued by Father Weigel and others. See, for example, John J. Wright, "Catholics and Anti-Intellectualism," *Commonweal*, December 16, 1955, pp. 275-278, and Thomas O'Dea, *American Catholic Dilemma* (New York: Sheed and Ward, 1959).

[39] *Negro Press Digest*, April 28, 1964, pp. 4-5.

evidence of the advantages in at least one sector of the economy of increased education as preparation for even more advanced positions, government may encourage the development of skills in the Negro community that is, in fact, the requisite of any real, sustained economic improvement for any underprivileged group.

It can be seen that a truly self-generating cycle has been operating, {64} one that must be broken. Political impotence and the lack of social power are reflected in the absence of prominent officeholders. This absence is noted by the community generally, but especially by Negro youth who see no point in investing financially and psychically in further education. Lack of education is reflected in a paucity of candidates for office. Absence of officeholders means lessened social power. In this cycle, the presence or absence of officeholders is the crucial element, the psychological payoff, the point most amenable to change and most productive of further changes. In a sense it adds another dimension to the concept of "representative bureaucracy"—for the conferral of office demonstrates something about the values and standards of, and opportunities afforded by, the greater community. Bureaucracies, then, constitute a two-way street; their functions of representation are not limited to the mirroring of the community in the administrative process. Bureaucracies by their very structure represent truths about the nature of the societies they administer and the values that dominate them.

In sum, we can distinguish four intertwined meanings of that somewhat vague rubric *representative bureaucracy*. The most obvious is the simple representational notion that all social groups have a right to political participation and to influence. The second can be labeled the functional aspect;[40] the wider the range of talents, types, and regional and family contacts found in a bureaucracy, the more likely it is to be able to fulfill its functions, with respect to both internal efficiency and social setting. Bureaucracies also symbolize values and power realities and are thus representational in both a political and an analytic sense. Therefore, finally, social conduct and future behavior in a society may be channelized and encouraged through the mere constitution of the bureaucracy.

---

[40] For a discussion of the distinction see my *The Supreme Court in the Political Process* (New York: Macmillan, 1965), p. 30.

4
Merit, Civil Rights, and Civil Service

I

{65}
PERHAPS the most remarkable aspect of American attitudes toward merit in employment has been their naïveté and simplicity of approach. The significant fact is that "the dog did not bark in the night." Little examination of the problems in selection and promotion of the "most qualified" is to be found in the scholarly literature.

As Plato has demonstrated, rendering each man his due can be a comprehensive—if Delphic—standard for a reconstruction of society, with surprising applications that suggest so much while solving so little. Yet the principle Plato considered the ultimate, if unachievable, perfect standard Shakespeare saw as overly harsh and even threatening: "Use every man after his desert, and who should 'scape whipping?" So the problem is one of balancing generosity and judgment.

Where specific situations and their known requirements are considered some precision is possible in applying the standard of merit, but seldom to the degree assumed by most personnel officials. A job is not merely a situation and a prospective role is generally not fully detailed. Even the simplest job has multi-faceted aspects, many not anticipated, Of course certain aspects of a position will be precisely known. These in turn may be precisely measurable or relatively ascertainable, Specific performance—say, in the operation of a machine or in completing some specified units of work during a given period of time—then could {66} constitute a fairly precise demonstration of skill or its absence and could be tested to determine merit.

Another level of performance-connected merit involves "intangible" factors—judgment in crisis, innovating ability, and the like—incalculable as a rule with respect both to the expected performance of the individual and to the weight such factors will actually have in a position. We cannot precisely determine how creative a designer will be in the future, and very often we are unable to say with surety that the same amount of innovation as has in the past been required for a position will be necessary in the future. An established company may go on in channelized routines, requiring no innovative thinking on the part of its employees; or it may suddenly be faced with a challenge to its position, necessitating the exercise of great resourcefulness and creativity.

Continuous efforts are being made to categorize the less routine aspects of positions in order to permit evaluation. (Studies of military leadership in World War II gave special impetus to these efforts.) Factor-analytic techniques provide a means of analyzing the needs experienced in a position in the past, and even a basis for venturesome extrapolation of needs in the future. Students of the problem of personnel analysis are constantly engaged in creating more precise techniques for prediction of job needs as well as for analysis of performance so as to reduce the area of subjective evaluation. At the same time technological developments seem to enhance the need for creativity and other less routine, less testable, attributes for many positions.

Other factors that must be taken into account in a discussion of merit are characterological traits. For example, reliability and punctuality are often intimately related to performance. These traits may be deducible from past experience but are not always clearly measurable. They often involve matters which, with respect to at least some positions, are regarded as "strictly private" and outside the bounds of necessary scrutiny for a job. Extramarital sexual behavior is regarded as not relevant to the job performance of a factory worker although it would be relevant for a minister, a diplomat, a policeman on the vice squad, and even possibly for a movie or television producer. Punctuality is rather more important to an assembly-line worker than to creative craftsmen or salesmen. There are frequent disagreements about the extent of permissible inquiry with regard to these factors, yet it is clear that many {67} of them will in practice be "performance oriented" and will discriminate as to ability to perform a specific function successfully. In this sense, they are related to merit.

In some notable instances, however, the society excludes them from consideration of merit on grounds of public policy—even though it can be demonstrated that there is a connection (in many cases a vague one) between these qualities and expected performance in a position. For example, a person going through a divorce is more of a risk to an employer than one who has a stable family life; yet in most situations it would be regarded as unsportsmanlike to punish an applicant for such a complication of his "private" life; in the public service a standard excluding an applicant with a "personal" problem of this sort would arouse public antipathy and would almost certainly be thrown out in any court test.

In addition to factors which relate to individual performance in connection with some requirement of a job, there are a whole series of factors, which we shall call "extrinsic," that concern advantages or disadvantages, apart from abilities, an individual may have in dealing with others. He may, for example, be able to utilize familial background or long experience and friendship with others; the use of "connections" is commonplace in such diverse fields as insurance salesmanship, the law, and public relations. Again, a stunningly beautiful secretary may be regarded as a business asset, although her ability in stenography may or may not be positively correlated with such physical appearance. Similarly it has been suggested that there is an "executive type" with a characteristic appearance and manner who is much sought after in business corporations which largely run themselves. On the other hand, a woman in a "man's position," a member of a racial minority in a position which automatically labels him as "uppity," a hunchback as a receptionist—all meet different types of social resistance. The legitimacy of such resistance is difficult to evaluate precisely but it affects achievement and therefore "merit." Reaction of others is a consideration which can affect both the outcome of one's effort and the environment *in* which one must make that effort. Such extrinsic factors also include the acceptability of a person socially. It is clear that in our society Negroes are handicapped in their ability to move freely in various circles of the white community and to engage in certain forms of social activity. This is especially true in certain parts of the country.

{68} All the aspects of "merit" so far discussed relate to expected future achievement; presumably this is what is normally meant by "universalistic" criteria—a classification which, as we have seen, is both vaguer and more value-laden than is commonly recognized by its utilizers. But these are not the only considerations that in fact enter into calculations about a person's acceptability for a position.

Past achievement may be a measure of future effort, but it is also true that positions are awarded for past efforts without expectation of future achievement. A promotion may be a reward for enduring the drudgery of the past, intended perhaps to operate as an incentive to others. Indeed, achievement as a criterion for reward is solidly based not only in this society, but in others; it has been underestimated as a basis of social differentiation by even so brilliant and trenchant a writer as Weber.

One may separate out two types of achievement—achievement intimately connected with the workings of the unit and achievement for its own sake. It is the latter that is most frequently and easily recognized. He deserves a chance at the higher position who has labored for twenty-five years at the lower. The principle of seniority is grounded in part on the usefulness of having a rule to dispose arbitrarily of a matter that would otherwise be controversial, but it is also recognition of the elemental claim of effort, preferably unusually onerous or protracted or, less frequently, specially skillful; Eastern and Western civilizations alike admit the validity of this claim.

But recognition of the claim of past achievement as merit also has utility for the unit in which the individual is employed. As I have suggested, a promotional system is in part a morale builder, a way of promising eventual accommodation for those at the bottom of the ladder. It may also be a means for securing more intense devotion during the years before promotion, or for encouraging the taking on of onerous tasks which otherwise would seem not worth the trouble. Hence ascriptions of "merit" to individuals who have complied with the needs of the organizational unit are utilitarian and logical. But they represent as well a dimension of reward on the whole independent of predicted performance in the position at hand. Such discounting of future activity as a standard is pressed not only by the immediate unit involved but also on a larger scale by other agencies in the society, and indeed by the society itself.

{69} So intergovernmental transfer for promotion based upon seniority achieved in another unit bumping occurs up and down the line in any bureaucracy. Again, a social policy of rewarding veterans is in part premised upon the notion that the veterans have made a sacrifice for the larger unit the society and should have their reward even at the cost of some diminution of efficiency in, let us say, a local post office.

The intrusion of such extra-task considerations upon the standards for employee selection is a necessary concomitant of organizational behavior. That is to say, the puristic stand that there should be individual merit unrelated to any social consideration is unrealistic, for there is no such thing as a position outside of the general system in which it operates. We have here the personnel director's analogue of Lincoln's problem: "shall one law be preserved and the Constitution fail?"

In the federal service extraneous social standards are reflected in the requirement that certain individuals be hired though they may not be the best qualified for the position (e.g., veterans preference, as we have already noted) and in the consideration given to social benefits and welfare needs (e.g., creation of extra jobs, not justified by the work load, in depressed areas). Federal service standards also ignore certain factors (in addition to some of the "private" considerations already mentioned) that could influence the effectiveness of performance but are held to be " intrinsically" irrelevant to the job—regardless of how much they are in fact involved. Such matters as religion, sex, and race are potentially related to performance, but by and large society feels it cannot afford to consider them as relevant and therefore the government is forbidden to use them as criteria in employment. They may still enter the selection process to a slight degree; a woman can be excluded from a heavy laborer's job without stirring up too much excitement. But for the run-of-the-mill job, sex must be disregarded.[1] This attitude is not limited to governmental employment, We insist that some considerations be ignored even by private parties. Most conspicuous are the comparatively recent fair employment practices regulations.[2] But {70} traditionally the courts have always taken various facets of "public policy" into account in interpreting contracts, in regulating unions, and the like; this has had an effect similar to fair employment regulations—the elimination of considerations which some would like to apply and which might marginally, or even to a significant

---

[1] In fall 1965 the Equal Employment Opportunity Commission experienced considerable difficulties in determining the line between permissible and impermissible in employment on the basis of sex. Earlier the New York World's Fair was forced to discontinue advertisements for blonde guides. *New York Times*, April 14,1965, p. 24.

[2] *First Report, Fair Employment Practice Committee, July 1943–December 1944* (1945), pp. 148-149.

extent, affect efficiency on the job. What seems to be taking place is a sort of balancing of interests in which the societal interest in maintaining peace and tranquility—the morale of society—is weighed against the right of the employer, individual or governmental, to apply relevant standards to his prospective employees. In this balancing, certain standards, even though relevant, may be ruled out if their effect is to diminish the general social tranquility.

It has been traditional to separate from universalistic, objective "merit considerations" particularistic considerations under the heading of "status" considerations. The suggestion here is that there are, in fact, two different types of status or particularistic standards: rough standards somewhat inefficiently linked to performance—those we shall designate as "echelon" merit[3]—and those that are in fact unrelated to performance at all.

Many societies utilize shorthand classifications which have some relevance to possible performance perhaps as a social convenience in communication, perhaps as a simple method of disposing of the complex problem of allocation of position and role. For example, educational degrees do not truly differentiate individuals by intelligence and learning, even in a fairly small society. In a complex society where there are multitudinous institutions with numerous teachers of varying standards, the meaning of an educational degree becomes even less standardized. Nonetheless, such a classification is intended to be related to both past achievement and potential growth: However low the correlation between potential for performance and the obtaining of degrees, the fact remains that it is almost certainly a positive one. Similarly with regard to the achievement of specialist standing in a field such as medicine, or even more strikingly, accounting; the standard requirement is that one pass through a series of tests related to knowledge and achievement which, {71} presumably, have a high correlation with future achievement. But before one can take these tests one must have passed a sequence of earlier tests, which imposes a pattern of time-serving that may or may not be relevant to future achievement. That is to say, there is no way in which one can readily short-circuit the system; one must rather move gradually up the rungs regardless of one's merit at the particular moment in time. Such echelon arrangements, when well calibrated, also serve the function we have previously noted of adjusting the mutual needs of individual advancement and maintenance of morale of other participants in the total system.

All of this is quite sharply differentiated from another type of generalized attribution of "merit" which is independent of performance, past or future. Although ability as a criterion may be pressed into service in situations of

---

[3] This category was suggested by Erving Goffman's rather different concept of "echelon control." See *Asylums* (New York: Anchor Books, 1961), p. 42. The limitations of echelon merit as an accurate discriminant are suggested in the modern Jewish "folk saying," "A Phudnick is a nudnick with a Ph.D.," or the more authentic "You can send an ox around the world but he still comes back an ox."

severe attack on prerogatives, the nobility generally assert a right to positions simply because of nobility. That is to say, only under duress—when prerogatives themselves appear in real danger—is the assertion made that in fact the nobility or the gentry can perform certain functions on the average better than others. Under extreme conditions even the most particularistic considerations are passed off as echelon arrangements. But in the normal course of events claims of the nobility are made in terms of criteria extrinsic to performance. So it is not surprising to find that the British in the nineteenth century, as noted in the previous chapter, actually gave preference to incompetents within the nobility on the grounds that they had a need which the state could satisfy. The special claims of gentlemen were met if they had no way of satisfying those claims through ordinary social life. This eleemosynary concept was the epitome of the strictly particularistic claim.[4]

Similarly the most charismatic claim—the claim of anointment by God himself—has built into it no necessary appeal to effectiveness. The test of merit is not expectation of success in the performance of a role, or function, for God's ways are wonderful; no one may know what His purposes are except through revelation, which is not generally an efficiency criterion. Claims of inheritance, ethical worthiness, or predestination, in short, do not rest upon any expectation of performance and are truly "particularistic." But even they, as we have noted, will tend to be {72} restated in a form oriented toward performance if they come under heavy attack.

In summary then, there are several levels of criteria related to job specification. and job performance. The first level is a consideration of *what is specifically required of the man by the job*. The second level concerns *what the man will be asked to do under less well defined circumstances*. Then the question becomes one of expectancies about the application of the man's skill to the situation—*what in fact he will do*, given the conditions. There is here ambiguity both in regard to the man's own potential and in regard to the environment that is created for him to work in. The next level, that of social acceptability, relates to *how a man will fit in*. Yet another level deals with the problem of *what a man has accomplished*, and the final consideration boils down to what are the side effects of his being given the position, *how others will react*, the effect upon the achievement of others.

While it is sometimes useful, as well as usual, to think of some of these considerations as being job-related, universalistic criteria and those of a different order as outside-the-job, irrelevant, particularistic claims, in actual fact there is no such sharp, clear line. As Blau comments, amplifying some recent observations by Parsons, the redefinition of a unit in which a job is located or of the goals attributed to the unit also alters what is an objective consideration for that job. There is, therefore, an infinite series of "nesting"

---

[4] J. Donald Kingsley, *Representative Bureaucracy* (Yellow Springs, Ohio: Antioch Press, 1944), pp. 28-30.

categories in reference to each of which a specific standard may be regarded as universalistic or particularistic, depending upon its neighbors against which we contrast the criterion.[5] This is in part a consequence of using a simple-minded, dichotomy but also a consequence of shifting standards of relevance. It would appear that this is basically a logical consequence of a lack of sharp boundaries to social units, while goals attributed to such units are in any event largely artificial constructs of the observer.

II

The ability of any structure and its component members to gain control over a definition of its boundaries and purposes can be regarded as a benchmark of its social power. Absolute control in these matters {73} would amount to something like "sovereignty" in the mystical sense in which that term was commonly utilized in pre-World War I and, alas, sometimes even in post-World War II political science.

The ability of business enterprise in the heyday of laissez faire to assert its fiscal purposes as paramount, to the exclusion of all other considerations, constitutes a remarkable chapter in the history of institutions. Thus Henry Ford could, in a classical example, entice thousands of semi literates to come to work for him from hundreds of miles outside the Detroit area, utilize their services when it was convenient for him, and lay off the workers whenever it suited his profit. All of this was done without consideration of the social consequences; nor did Ford feel it necessary to make restitution for the burdens put upon the community by his actions. In short, the definition by commercial enterprise of its employees' need, fitness, and merit was virtually absolute. This power was only achieved by simultaneously restricting the goals of such an enterprise, interpretation of which was then left completely to the individual enterprise. As Adolph Berle points out, the business corporation was by law enjoined to maximize profits and to heed no other criterion of action. Any other consideration—welfare of employees, for example—was illicit if it did not contribute to increased profits.[6] Nevertheless industry was not completely insulated from broad common-law standards even in this period; in selection of personnel as in other areas the standards of "public policy," vague as they were, were clearly operative. And the history of legal developments in the United States in this century has, of course, been an assertion of the right of society to insist that a company consider not only its ledger but the broader consequences of its actions.

---

[5] Peter Blau, *Exchange and Power in Social Life* (New York; Wiley, 1965), p. 38. Blau credits Talcott Parsons and Robert F. Bales, *Family, Socialization and Interaction Process* (New York: Free Press, 1955), pp. 117-118, 161-466, with suggesting this point.

[6] A. A. Berle, Jr., *The Twentieth Century Capitalist Revolution* (New York Harvest Books, 1954), pp. 166-169.

Similarly, the professions have been entrusted with striking autonomy over personnel selection, largely unreviewed and basically discretionary. But they have given significant hostages to fate in their concession that their goals are in fact social and even largely socially defined. Their actions, therefore, particularistically formulated and perhaps even motivated in the same manner), must always be articulated in the most universalistic of terms and are tested by the criteria of ultimate social benefits. The right of redefinition of purpose is dearly granted to the community—a fact which may well explain the intensity {74} with which even minor alterations in the relationship are fiercely resisted, especially by the medical profession, which does not wish the community to get into the habit of such redefinition.

The absence, then, of purely logical formulation of relevant criteria for personnel recruitment is a source of political uncertainty and has its political uses. To a large extent social convention, the outcome of past political struggles, determines present arrangements. These arrangements are seen as logical," even inevitable, as they become sanctified with age. But the logic is seldom so overwhelming that a group experiencing new social power is unable to formulate new "logical" propositions and press its claims for what it comes to regard as truly—as opposed to pseudo—universalistic and appropriate standards in employment.

Broader definition of the implications of decision, of the goals or purposes that prove and justify the standards for employee selection, is only one aspect of the situation. The process of recruitment itself becomes involuted and complex as well. Strictly speaking, maximization of "equal opportunity," a vigorous application of merit considerations, requires not only that the standard of selection be objectively related to bringing forward the best person, but also that there be equal access to the selection process, including widespread availability of information. Neither is, of course, a sufficient condition for genuine equality of opportunity, but rather both are dearly necessary.

The opening up of recruiting channels is neither easy nor simple. To put it more directly, the problem of equalizing conditions resembles that of maintaining a footing on quicksand. A superbly qualified candidate who is in the process of getting a new pair of glasses may miss sufficient questions in a test to be edged out by another. Another candidate may be delayed in getting to the testing place and thus be nervous as well as ten minutes tardy upon arrival. If we allow for such circumstances, where do we stop? Should we include general emotional stress? What of past records of experience with tests? Do we take into consideration the social and educational opportunities that have been afforded the individuals and their ancestors? These are not merely questions of what is best for the individual—although perhaps in some moral sense his "worth" is indeed best expressed as a quotient of his achievements over his potentialities. But even from the organizational standpoint, it seems reasonable to give some consideration to the potential {75} for growth indicated in such a record. If an applicant who was forced out of school for financial reasons at the ninth-grade level scores equally well on information and cultural sophistication as a college graduate—a Phi Beta Kappa to boot—this would in most instances be evidence of remarkable intelligence and drive in the educationally deprived man.[7]

If one applies such considerations, social and cultural, to broader social groupings, the matter becomes even more complex. "Availability" is not a simple fact in an industrial community. "Roundabout" development of human resources may be even more distinctive a characteristic of modern society than "roundabout" production of material goods. Recruitment for positions is enmeshed in social relationships of various kinds—as simple a matter as a neighbor informing another of a vacancy in her office or as complex a matter as the civil service recruiter visiting his own alma mater yearly compared with a biennial trip to other colleges. But in a larger sense recruitment for decisional, technical, and professional positions is a process of development of conduits—complex patterns of education, acquaintanceship, and apprenticeship—that reach back practically speaking almost to birth.

III

A federal executive attempting to implement the equal employment program, who conscientiously examines its implications, is forced into an awareness of a long trail, with many possible detours. He may begin by merely taking the lordly position that he will evaluate objectively applicants who present themselves before him, but if he is truly conscientious he will go on to examine recruitment policies in order to make sure that they give more than lip service to the quest for equality. He may decide to do what many fellow executives have done: dispatch recruiters to Negro colleges in the South, once so infrequently visited by government recruiters. (Some southern Negro colleges have had to build interviewing facilities in the wake of changed federal policies.) Recruitment through office gossip can be supplemented by the official posting of notices of vacancies in places where potential Negro applicants will see them. Positive publicity can be channeled to the Negro press, and so on.

Further soul searching may result in reopening the question of proper definition of qualifications in terms of their actual application to performance on the job as well as in terms of possible racial discrimination in the testing process. An executive who recognizes that the opportunities for gaining the necessary qualifications may themselves be imbedded in discriminatory patterns may even delve into remote aspects of social relationships.

A truly sensitive administrator thus tackling the apparently simple problem of expanding opportunity for employment can find himself driven to

---

[7] "...I contend that a Negro candidate who makes 115 on an aptitude test is likely to be just as bright if not a whole lot smarter than the white fellow who scores 125," Whitney Young, Jr., *To Be Equal* (New York McGraw-Hill, 1964), p. 63.

constant examination of the whole network of selection and the entire philosophical problem of merit. In practice he must draw the line somewhere, decide that total redress of the balance of social wrongs is beyond his power. The subjectivity of that line—along with the sheerly human necessity for drawing it—constitutes the justification and rationalization for any level of activity or inactivity on the part of the administrator. He can at any of the various levels justify his behavior as being what he himself considers desirable and practical. And the statistical result in employment—the ratio of Negroes to whites in his agency, for example—may be quite logically defended by an executive at any of these levels as caused by and explicable by forces other than those operating within the agency.

The challenge of the civil rights movement to past practice in the federal service has two facets in relation to the merit system. Insofar as it stresses elimination of artificial barriers, the movement enforces the principles of the merit system and reduces dissonance between articulated values and actual practice for the bureaucracy.[8] Indeed, current procedures designed to eliminate discrimination are a "confession in avoidance" for some, and an even more direct admission of past discrimination for others. But insofar as the movement seeks to apply new standards to alter past patterns, it arouses fears in many defenders of the merit system. When leaders of civil rights groups speak of "compensatory employment" or "benign quotas" they evoke absolute hostility.[9] More conservative forces have already utilized the slogan "reverse {77} discrimination" and argue that Negroes are already a privileged rather than a deprived minority.[10]

Such "favoritism" can rationally be defended, as an influential recent analysis by Charles Silberman reminds us.[11] The state of Israel, setting out systematically to raise the cultural level of her Near Eastern and North African Sephardi majority to that of her citizens of Western derivation, not only has launched a massive educational program, but actually has set different standards of educational achievement for these two sub-communities. There are lower standards for the Sephardim, for both admission to schools and qualifying for state financial support toward higher education. There is a

---

[8] Personnel officers, in assessing utilization of Negro skills, have perforce had to give more than lip service to the upgrading of skills of all personnel. In many of my interviews the new-found talents of employees were mentioned with obvious satisfaction and personal pride by personnel officers.

[9] See Robert Carter et al., *Equality* (New York: Pantheon Books, 1965), especially the discussion by Peter Marcuse, pp. 154ff. But as Carter himself observes, p. 102, "Negroes themselves can only be ambivalent at best about benign quotas."

[10] In 1963 hearings on "reverse discrimination" in the technical violation of rules in promotion of postal workers in Dallas were held by the House Committee on the Post Office and Civil Service. Replies to periodic inquiries to the committee have indicated the hearings will eventually be published.

[11] Charles E. Silberman, *Crisis in Black and White* (New York: Vintage, 1984), pp. 275-285.

political motivation at work here: concessions are more likely to be given to a restive majority than to a militant minority, as in the United States. Basically, however, the differential standards were instituted and are maintained on the theory that they more or less equalize acquired inequalities, on the order of a golf handicap or weight differentials compensating for jockeys' bulk in racing. In time, it is hoped, such handicaps will not be necessary, but for now they introduce a certain amount of social stability as well as augment the cultural level of the deprived majority.

In the United States libertarian groups increasingly, though still guardedly, press demands for compensatory preference. To put the matter figuratively, we cannot with justice say to a man compelled to carry a burden on his back for a long way in a race, and therefore miles behind, "You may drop the pack; the race is now equal." Amends must be made because of the past discrimination.[12]

IV

Claims for compensation usually take the form of demands for special governmental programs and concerted expenditures for the special benefit of the Negro community. But here it is not necessary to call for compensation, for there is a much better criterion—the simple one of {78} need, Compensatory arguments are more usually invoked on behalf of the Negroes among the qualified individuals applying for a position. Quotas are seldom urged for their own sake, but more as proof of the fact that discrimination has ended. "I merely ask that the placement officers use the same ingenuity today in bringing the Negro up as they once used in holding him down," as one civil rights leader has explained. But lurking only slightly beneath the surface is the implication that artificial and discriminatory, perhaps even unconsciously derived, standards, rather than true merit, have been controlling in the past throughout the federal service; therefore, some urge, new standards favoring those previously discriminated against are in order. Further, since most of the positions in governmental service require minimum not maximum capabilities, advocates of "favoritism" argue, reserving specific positions for a disadvantaged racial group would not hinder most functions of the government, and indeed would be hardly noticed at all. Since the indices currently used for determining merit are culturally imposed and are often irrelevant to the basic duties of the position, considerable leeway does in fact exist here.

The principle of compensation for a minority is, however, a voracious one that knows no limit and demands almost abject psychological acceptance among the majority. Reparation for past injustice by means of wide-scale

---

[12] The metaphor appears independently in two articles in the same journal: Joseph Robison, "Giving Reality to the Promise of Job Equality," *Law in Transition Quarterly*, 1: 104-117 (1964), and Richard Lichtman, "The Ethics of Compensatory Justice," 1: 76-103.

voluntary allocation of jobs and positions is a program that would apparently be unprecedented in world history. Role allocations in society are not normally made according to such a principle, for the compensation so involved would of course be indeterminate in amount and duration; only an overweening force has usually been sufficient to exact this kind of payment. The compensationist wing of the civil rights movement argues with cogency that the indefiniteness of the amount of compensation is appropriate; for, as the compensationists point out, the damages extend far back in time and are themselves vague and almost unending in their ramifications. But a cogent argument does not always win in the realm of reality, Further, this argument contains within it weaknesses. Acceptance of its implications by the majority would be akin to ultimate abnegation. What position in society would be exempt? What handicap would constitute an unreasonable obstacle to the occupying of any position desired? What of other disabilities should they not be rewarded? The continuously deprived, the army of Lee Harvey Oswald's, certainly the Indians, the {79} shy, perhaps the brunettes who have less fun, can all press claims to compensation for past disadvantages. The horrible specter of a Cave of Adullam bargaining for special advantages is sufficient deterrent to such a sharp departure from the traditional merit system. As with the claims of special groups for augmented political strength through malapportionment, the strongest argument against compensatory preference is simply that the claim is insufficiently self-containing and self-defining to be satisfied without continuous social strife. The remedy is far worse than the disease.

The heart of the compensationist dilemma is found buried in a 28-page discussion of "The Ethics of Compensatory Justice" by a member of the staff of the Center for the Study of Democratic Institutions: "For if the Negro has been denied that very characteristic—merit—upon which employment is to be distributed, then he has equally well been denied the other goods which are dependent upon his position in employment. He cannot now enjoy those goods equally with the remainder of the community through the single device of future nondiscrimination."[13] While Mr. Lichtman quickly runs away from his own discovery of the lack of real limits to the compensationist claim by pointing out that merit is more crucial in some positions than others, and that it is not precisely ascertainable, he cannot escape the consequence of asserting that merit in his scheme should be irrelevant.

He argues that a white employee who would be injured by preference shown to a Negro is not being punished: "What he undergoes is not punishment, in any strict sense of that term, but the removal from an unfair advantage to which he is not entitled.... Whites who ask why they are to be dismissed must be confronted plainly with the fact that it is as a result of an

---

[13] Lichtman, "The Ethics of Compensatory Justice," *Law in Transition Quarterly*, 1: 97.

Merit, Civil Rights and Civil Service

unjust procedure that they have been hired. A given white who asks why *he* is to be dismissed must be referred to some characteristic which separates him from other whites—length of service, competence, need, etc.—or to chance. Both chance and discriminatory exclusion deny a man employment. But it cannot be ignored that the one does so impartially, and the other, immorally."[14] Aside from whether socially existent statuses are so easily upset without severe social costs (one might imagine what Mr. Lichtman would have {80} to say about the displacement of workers by automation) it is clear that this position evades the central point—that an individual will refuse to be categorized only in relation to other whites, but will persist in asking about his merit in relation to the Negro. He who steps forward to re-establish justice where injustice lay has a responsibility, at least in the common law, to *see* that the new situation he creates is better than the old one. This standard is clearly not met by most of the compensatory suggestions, of which Mr. Lichtman's remains, to my knowledge, the clearest and the most straightforward. The principle of collective guilt that underlies the compensatory arguments is very difficult to accept, and not all whites are willing to take up a burden to compensate for the one the Negro bore for so long. Every man bears his own burden, and every man tends to regard it as extremely weighty. One is tempted to cite exceptional cases like the recent instance of a deaf genius who was classified as mentally retarded until his intelligence level was accidentally discovered in his eighteenth year. Even where the burden is not obvious, whites will not readily admit that their own particular background gives them such an unfair advantage that they should bear a pronounced and unmeasurable handicap throughout their lives.

The situation is different when it can be shown that a direct advantage is clearly the result of discrimination. So, for example, there is clear justification for the recent efforts of the Equal Employment Opportunity Commission to abolish separate ratings for equal work and to see to it that in the fusion of seniority lines Negroes do not go to the bottom of the white list, but take the place they would have had if there had, been one seniority line when they were hired. The sole advantage that a white man hired a day after a Negro has had in the past has been due to the separate seniority lines; the merging should end the advantage so gained. Similar applications of this principle will end a good deal of existing discrimination against Negroes, so that the trauma of merging lines will not have to be repeated.

In the short run, where performance differences are small and the job itself is not crucial, it has always been possible to set aside merit criteria and to admit the principle of need. Here the compensationists suggest that quotas might well be invoked as an effective way of meeting the problem of Negro employment. The difficulty on the governmental level is that in terms of

---

[14] *Ibid.*, pp. 98-99.

absolute numbers the Negro is already {81} overrepresented in the federal service. Presumably, there might be insistence upon quotas for Negroes at higher levels, and in different positions. But eventually such quotas would cut the other way and work to the disadvantage of the Negro. As more Negroes become better qualified a quota system would actually force them into competition with each other instead of permitting competition among all qualified Negroes and whites for all available jobs.

In the immediate future the issue is not critical, particularly if a formula can be arrived at for the weighting of such quotas in objective fashion, removed from political whim. But in the long run such arrangements are sources of friction, probably beyond their advantage. At the present time the principle of representativeness operates as a moral check upon the operations of the bureaucracy at least, and provides a yardstick more flexible and not less telling than any quota arrangement. That is to say, an administrator can always check his performance against what logic and the distribution of the population would suggest, and thus usually find himself failing. In this respect the United States has probably been more successful with its implicit quota based upon population than the Indian government with a rigid quota written into its constitutional provisions.

There are, in any event, many substitutes for direct and overt compensation. No stigma of individual guilt or loss attaches itself to programs designed to improve the lot of the Negro through mass expenditures or programs granting educational advantages to them. But the fact is that in the field of education, preference to Negroes has so far been resisted perhaps even more than preference in the field of employment, Pressure for educational advantages has not come from the Negro community, and the advantages of the moment are not sufficient to warrant excessive agitation on the part of civil rights advocates, but any long-run solution would clearly have to be based on special educational efforts. So far the compensationists have been too concerned with short-run problems to have moved in this direction,

The traditional argument for civil rights has been that the Constitution is color blind. Compensationists argue that the ignoring of this rule in the past requires that it be ignored at least temporarily in the future. The moral position is debatable, but the practical consequences of the argument in terms of the law are on the whole not readily acceptable. The problem is that what Herbert Wechsler calls "neutral principles," {82} or general norms that go beyond the immediate standards of the particular law, are created by such actions. If the law may regularly take into account color for benevolent purposes, it is difficult to see why color is not relevant with respect to matters where liabilities would result from its consideration. To be blunt about it, if prejudice is a criterion for favoring the Negroes, then there are many areas where a social policy of discrimination could be based upon the existence of prejudice, It is for this reason that Carter found ambivalence among Negroes on the use of any quota arrangement.[15] The tradition of the common law, at least its nominal values, dates back to the political theory of Hooker, Locke, and Hobbes, who insisted that equality was a great simplifying assumption for society. It is not the reality of equal worth that concerns individuals and the law; it is the fact that any other assumption generates dilemmas. These are easily avoided by eliminating all efforts to ascertain inequalities legally. We may then socially. individually, morally, ethically, and compensatorily act to achieve as much justice as we can.

No writer has bettered Aristotle's suggestion that injustice consists of treating equals inequitably or those not equals identically. Advocates of the extreme civil rights position wish to go beyond surface equality to give the Negro a reward proportionate to some hidden worth. Echelon preference for Negroes is conceived of as righting a wrong; all Negroes should obtain a benefit, for all Negroes have equally suffered as a group, as an echelon. But how much preference is the proper amount? For which positions does the handicap apply and for which would it be excluded—and on what principle? What is the evidence that a particular applicant suffered specific deprivation beyond the general and indisputable fact of universal Negro mistreatment? What evidence is there that the specific deprivation would have affected his {83} performance on this particular job? These questions suggest, too, that the adoption of a clearly non-job-connected criterion threatens the total operation of the general principle of merit, and may lead to new justifications for job preference that are in fact detrimental simply because of the time and effort that would be consumed in their evaluation. One must remember that a criterion for selection for a position should be such as to minimize the costs of ascertaining fitness wherever possible. If the costs in obtaining information exceed the advantages accruing in the selection of the individual, then the criterion would on the whole be rejected.[16]

Consideration of these and, related social and logical arguments has led civil rights groups to assert much vaguer and less provocative claims—claims which can be more easily met and which are more compatible with the norms of civil service as a whole. Demands for better tests, for standards of selection

---

[15] Veterans preference throughout history has evoked opposition from civil service advocates and personnel specialists precisely for this reason—because of the sapping of the operating principles of the merit system, rather than because of any demonstrated decline in governmental efficiency that ensues. As Walter Seal Carpenter has pointed out, veterans preference actually antedates the concept of merit and is probably more deeply rooted in popular sentiment. *The Unfinished Business of Civil Service Reform* (Princeton, N.J.: Princeton University Press, 1952), pp. 11-14. Yet civil service advocates have never really accommodated to its demands. In contrast to civil rights supporters, veterans present specific claims based on individual experience, are drawn from the total community (which makes the preference less "inherently challenging"), and are at any one time in history claiming benefits for one generation—happily for the demanders, their own rather than for an indefinite and undefinable future.

[16] Carter *et al.*, *Equality*, p. 102.

that are more clearly related to job necessity and less to what the middle class regards as "nice things to know," for open recruitment not co-optation all these are fully compatible with the strengthening rather than the weakening of the merit principle. There are many departments of the federal service that have yet to attempt seriously to implement such measures, so considerable progress can be made at this level alone, In addition the process of promotion, particularly to positions of responsibility at the higher reaches of the bureaucracy, is almost universally so infected with subtle personnel biases that great strides will be made as this process is rendered more objective, less susceptible to hidden prejudice. Subjective judgment can never be completely eliminated in performance evaluation except perhaps in evaluating the most menial and meaningless levels of skill, but it can be more disciplined. Here, too, civil rights leaders generally believe they should first "exhaust remedies" before making wider claims.

Arguments based upon the idea of "representative bureaucracy" can be pressed with vigor, particularly at the upper levels of the service, and with regard to elite and influential—policy-making structures, where Negroes have not been accorded and have not achieved strong representation. Job-related criteria can be invoked successfully here too in order to expand the role of the Negro. The advantages of his employment are often tangible and demonstrable. For example, greater {84} participation of Negroes in the Foreign Service would be beneficial simply by virtue of the physical appearance of Negroes as representatives of the United States in countries where the charge of discrimination is a propaganda weapon against this country. Such advantages would probably be reaped more abundantly in dealing with, say, student groups in Europe than in wooing the ephemeral officeholders in African countries, but the service so far has shown small recognition of this.[17]

Other representational arguments have similar and immediate relevance. The preceding chapter emphasized the desirability of broad participation of social groupings in policy-making in order to ensure articulation of diverse points of view, to encourage a sense of participation throughout the population, and to legitimize resultant policies by dispersing responsibility. None of these asserted conditions are fully realized in our major policy units; job-related advantages have been preferred at the expense of broad social needs.

Inasmuch as the practical advantages of making claims in terms of these less controversial standards are yet to be exhausted, more radical claims do not have to be pressed. In essence the civil rights advocates demand *preference* within the system, improvement of procedures, resolution of ambiguities in favor of Negroes, selection of Negroes where they are as well qualified as whites, or, very occasionally, selection at the lower levels of Negroes who are *sufficiently* qualified even when indices suggest a white candidate might be

---

[17] Richard Johnson, "The Representativeness of the American Foreign Service Officers Corps" (State Department report, undated, mimeographed), pp. 4-5.

slightly more qualified in ways deemed not absolutely necessary to the job.

At the same time, merit system advocates are willing to re-examine continuously the purity of the implementation of the standard of merit; in many ways it strengthens their hands to have political pressures brought upon them directed toward that end. For under the stress of such pressures they may be able to vindicate merit and to indicate the dangers of departure from such a standard. Thus they can effect desirable changes while pointing to the evils that would ensue from making concessions in response to other pressures than merit. They are on the whole quite willing to undertake vigorous recruitment drives, to open up new channels of recruitment, to diversify and enrich the service. Where there are candidates of equal rank they see no problem in taking {85} into account broader social categories, though they may blanch at passing over a candidate with a higher score for reasons other than demonstrated or indicated ability. In short, they are willing to give preference as long as it is *within* the system.

So an uneasy, unstable equilibrium exists. It is uneasy because new economic or demographic or political developments can easily lead to new more stringent and more vocal demands. It is unstable because it is not properly legitimized or internalized in the minds of either participating group. Both see problems that they think could easily be solved—but their solutions differ. So far the current situation is accepted because there is pragmatic movement in the direction desired by both; only time can tell whether that fortunate conjunction of interests will perdure.

5

Negro Employment, an Analysis

I

{86}
IN THE field of employment, as in housing, the Negro by and large is forced to take the leavings, to find what work he can in jobs that the dominant whites deem unattractive and that immigrant group after immigrant group has left behind after utilizing them as steppingstones to jobs presumed more lucrative and prestigious. The analogy to housing is even more exact; for when a Negro position begins to appear attractive for whatever change of mind or turn of the economy—the means for reclaiming it for white use have almost invariably been found.

The usual image of Negro employment—the last man hired, the first man fired—is accurate enough as far as it goes, But an image borrowed from the segregated bus is perhaps even more illuminating—it is certain that no better than "back of the bus" jobs will be available, but there is no boundary ensuring specific occupational places will be preserved for Negroes, who are instead allowed to advance or retreat at white convenience. An old sign on Oklahoma public transportation antedating the Supreme Court's anti-segregation decision appealed to whites to respect the line of demarcation and leave designated seats for Negroes on the grounds that "it's a poor rule that doesn't work both, ways." In employment as in public transportation, housing, and many other areas, the "rule" has clearly worked just one way.

{87} Broad types of discrimination in employment can be analyzed in logical categories, Indeed these approach a sociological scale. At the one extreme in its effect is the simple and total exclusion of all Negroes from a general area of employment. More usual is the Hamitic policy of reserving the more menial, onerous, and poorly paying posts for Negroes as befitting "hewers of wood and drawers of water." Segregated lines of employment may be maintained, with some overlap in duties and perhaps even in pay and responsibility, as is the situation with porters and conductors on trains.[1] Further along the scale, equal work may be classified and/or paid for in

---

[1] See Herman Miller, *Rich Man, Poor Man* (New York: Crowell, 1964), p. 91, and Dale Hiestand, *Economic Growth and Employment Opportunities for Minorities* (New York: Columbia University Press, 1964), pp. 2-5.

discriminatory fashion, A Negro "utility man" may be performing the same duties as a white "trucker," much as a woman "executive secretary" may have duties fungible with those of a male "administrative assistant." Perhaps the final point on the scale is reached when employment conditions are generally though imperfectly equal, but promotion, recognition, and increase in remuneration come more slowly for Negroes.

While these steps represent a gradation of discrimination in strictly logical terms, as the "objective" severity of the deprivation is altered, it is not clear that they represent steps of increasing acceptability to Negroes. It is clear that day-to-day tensions in employment are quite different from any linear projection of satisfaction, or indeed from the question of over-all satisfaction. One might easily argue that total exclusion would morally be more justifiable and less cynical than some of these more complex patterns of discrimination, much as current South African economic arrangements are in reality something quite different from and probably mare reprehensible, if one may use an old-fashioned term, than apartheid. We must distinguish between general satisfaction and tension levels, much as Samuel Stouffer in *The American Soldier* found it necessary to distinguish between over-all satisfaction with a position in the military and the existence of specific complaints. For example, in World War II, the military police, with a relatively glacial promotion schedule, had fewer individual grievances than Air Force personnel, who were conspicuously benefited by an advantageous table of organization. But when asked about over-all satisfaction the two groups reversed themselves. Air Force personnel were distinctly more {88} positive than MP's.[2] Although evidence is not overwhelming, what we do have points to an increase in Negro tension levels as their situation is objectively improved along the lines indicated above, but with a concomitant increase in over-all approval and understanding that they are indeed being benefited. Thus Negroes who are the bitterest and most tension-laden when given projection tests with regard to the civil rights situation are conspicuously more likely than Negroes displaying less tension to have white friends, to be interested in broader social questions, and to be positively related to the general community in attitude and interests. Thus improvement is indeed Janus-faced, and generates its own problems.[3]

The broad historical trends in Negro employment since emancipation can be summarized in brief compass. During the last half of the nineteenth century, Negroes were systematically forced from those few small-craft and relatively skilled positions that they had held as slaves, or as freed men in the

---

[2] Samuel A. Stouffer *et al.*, *The American Soldier* (Princeton, N.J.: Princeton University Press, 1949).

[3] Analogous conditions developed in Sicily where vigorous efforts to alleviate the economic situation produced a steady rise in the Communist vote.

cities, by economic pressure, legal disqualification, and labor union action.[4] Their success in small business was extremely limited, and confined largely to the servicing of their own community—funeral parlors, insurance and banking, and the like. In the professions also Negroes experienced success largely as functionaries for their own community with a preponderance of professional Negroes serving in the ministry, education, and the law, the verbal professions. Booker T. Washington urged his people to become proficient as agricultural technicians and skilled craftsmen. But agriculture had a drastic oversupply of personnel and there was no room for newcomers; neither was there any system of training open to Negroes wishing to become either technicians or craftsmen, and discriminatory laws, union constitutions, and franchises acted as further deterrents.[5]

The twentieth century has witnessed a significant out-migration of Negroes from the southern rural areas, "following the drinking gourd," first to southern and then to northern urban areas. While the overall migration of Negroes within the United States, except for brief periods like that of World War II, has generally been below that of the more mobile white population (see Table 1), the steady movement in one direction has had its effect in the remarkable transformation of a Negro rural majority, with many of the qualifies of a peasant class, into an overwhelmingly urban community of industrial proletarians. (See Table 2.) The percentage of urban Negroes now exceeds that of the nation as a whole. At the present time, the northern urban

Table 1. Percentage of Whites and Nonwhites Migrating between States in Selected Periods

Period	Whites	Nonwhites
1935–1940	5.5	3.9
1940–1947	9.7	14.1
1955–1960	9.2	6.1

SOURCE: Data from *The Economic Situation of Negroes in the U.S.*, U.S. Department of Labor Bulletin S-3, Revised, 1962, p. 2.

---

[4] See, for example, Richard B. Morris, *Government in Early American Colonies* (New York: Columbia University Press, 1946), pp. 182-188.

[5] See, for example, Herbert Hill, "The Racial Practices of Organized Labor in the Age of Gompers and After," in Arthur Ross and Herbert Hill, editors, *Employment, Race and Poverty* (New York: Harcourt, Brace and World, 1967).

Table 2. Percentage of Negroes in the South and in the Remainder of the United States, Urban and Rural Areas, 1900 and 1960

Area	1900	1960
United States	100.0	100.0
South	89.7	59.9
Urban	15.4	35.0
Rural	74.2	24.9
Remainder of the United States	10.3	40.1
Urban	7.2	38.2
Rural	3.1	1.9

SOURCE: Data from *The Economic Situation of Negroes in the U.S.*, U.S. Department of Labor Bulletin S-3, Revised, 1962, p. 2.

regions are the home of 40 percent, roughly, of the Negro population, while the majority of the remainder live in southern cities. Herman Miller, perhaps our leading census expert, predicts the situation will shortly stabilize with about 40 percent of the nation's Negro population remaining in the South.[6] Occupationally this transformation has meant that the majority have moved from agricultural service to industrial labor, but it opened the way to clerical and selling positions, especially for Negro women, as well as to industrial employment. Movement to the urban {90} North has also, however, had its adverse effects on the over-all employment picture for Negroes: it has somewhat weakened the monopoly on service to fellow Negroes that Negro small business men, teachers, and lawyers had at one time; and Negroes moving to the North have found themselves excluded from craft positions even more rigidly than in smaller southern cities where scattered craft occupations are traditionally held by Negroes. Thus, the escape routes for the Negro lower middle class are in fact even more restricted than in the past.

The lack of access to governmental positions over the years aggravated Negro problems. With the growth of governmental service that discrimination has loomed as an even more important factor in our society. The general growth of governmental service as a component of the total employment is reflected in Table 3.

---

[6] Miller, *Rich Man, Poor Man*, p. 213.

Table 3. Public Employment as a Percentage of the Labor Force from 1929 to 1962 (Selected Years)*

Year	Total Public Employment	Civilian Public Employment		
		Total	Federal Government	State and Local Governments
1929	6.7	6.2	1.1	5.1
1930	6.8	6.3	1.1	5.2
1933	6.6	6.1	1.1	5.0
1935	7.1	6.6	1.4	5.1
1939	7.8	7.2	1.6	5.6
1944	26.4	9.2	4.4	4.7
1949	12.0	9.2	3.0	6.2
1954	14.9	10.0	3.2	6.7
1959	14.9	11.4	3.1	8.3
1961	15.4	11.9	3.1	8.8
1962	16.1	12.3	3.1	9.2

SOURCE: U.S. Bureau of Labor Statistics, *Employment and Earnings Statistics*.
*Because of rounding, the figures for federal government and state-local government employment sometimes exceed the totals.

II

In a welfare state in which one out of eight employed persons (excluding the military) receives a government paycheck, state and federal policies loom as major determinants of job potential for Negroes.[7] In a warfare state in which an estimated six million workers are engaged in production under federal contracts, the economic leverage {91} of government particularly of federal defense policies for alleviation of discrimination in industry is immense. And in a personal service economy, which is likely to be the end-product of industrial automation, governmental employment seems certain to become one of the few potential growth areas for a job-starved minority, As Secretary of Labor Wirtz has pointed out, it is socially and politically easier to create new patterns of employment in sectors of the economy where there are new and additional jobs than to displace entrenched incumbents from job rights built upon traditional explicit or implicit discriminatory prerogatives. By 1963 nonwhite employment in civilian government service at all levels—national, local, state—had passed the one million mark.

---

[7] See Solomon Fabricant, *The Trend of Governmental Activity in the United States since 1900* (New York: National Bureau of Economic Research, 1952), pp. 3 and 25.

THE NEGRO IN FEDERAL EMPLOYMENT

Traditionally government has been regarded as a good employer for the Negro, but this is largely a reflection of the reputation of the federal service in recent times, and even here it has been a highly relative matter. The norms of equality and universalistic criteria for competence operated even in the late nineteenth century to mitigate the more extreme white supremacy notions in the federal civil service; it has been regarded as unthinkable that public service should be closed permanently to any group of citizens contributing tax dollars to its support, Yet even the national government has unmistakably, crudely, and blatantly ratified the class system of employment in various periods, and local government structures have gone so far as to exclude Negroes completely in a number of employment areas over scores of years.

Social scientists have utilized the social backgrounds of persons in power positions in various societies to answer questions about the distribution of power. The predominance of Great Russians in the USSR, for example, or of persons of Western European descent in American politics—as well as the recent dilution of that predominance—tells a great deal about the society's structure. The pronounced shift in the type of background of leaders in post-revolutionary, as opposed to Czarist, Russia, when compared with the minute differences among party leaders in the United States, or even in Great Britain, almost suggests a measuring rod of the degree of social cleavage and change in influence possible under different political systems.

If this type of crude measuring device is applied to nonwhites in government employment a rough picture of American society emerges. Nonwhites currently constitute about 12 percent of all government servants, federal, state, and local—a proportion slightly greater than {92} their proportion in the general population and about equal to their proportion in the labor force generally.[8] But as is commonly known, they have been preponderantly—up to a few years ago virtually exclusively—relegated to the lower rungs of the bureaucracy. Even in the higher status positions, nonwhites are concentrated in research or staff positions, largely in the area of intergroup relations, rather than in decision-making line posts. It is to the qualitative issue of type of position available to Negroes, as well as the quantitative issues of total numbers of Negroes, and status and income of their positions, that recent attention has been given. That pervasive discrimination has existed in the federal service is beyond question. Administrators freely admit this with exemplary candor, It was traditional until very recently for administrators to ascribe discriminatory practices to the past and claim complete eradication in the period in which they spoke. Now, even this evasiveness has been largely abandoned by most administrators in their attempt to do something about the problem.

The most thorough study of discrimination in the federal service—and

---

[8] *Ibid.*

one that unfortunately was never published—is the doctoral dissertation of the late William Bradbury, completed at Columbia University in 1952. This survey of federal practice in the immediate post-World War II era is a valuable benchmark for comparing the efficiency of current programs.[9]

Bradbury bad no trouble in obtaining anecdotal material on discrimination from Negro and white alike. His study records explicit recollections, such as the rebuke by superiors of white personnel officers for efforts to hire Negroes; provides a survey of Negro employment in the late 1940's—a one-man head count as it were; and also describes the experiences of wartime agencies in attempting to relocate their staff after the war. The CPA under Chester Bowles had been unusually open to Negro employment, particularly in the upper ranks, and the placement problems when the agency was dissolved were consequently greater than those of any of the other temporary agencies. It was the considered opinion of the executive in charge of this placement, expressed in a long, careful memo, that "We have not found a single agency in which there has been no evidence of racial discrimination."[10] {93} Degrees of prejudice varied enormously but obstacles were present everywhere.

Bradbury also essayed a more controlled study of whites and Negroes employed in one specific but unidentified operation, with close comparison of initial employment and rates of advancement for members of both races. The study indicates pretty much what Herman Miller's gross comparisons of Negro-white income have shown: that Negro college graduates have expectations no greater than whites who have completed the eighth grade,[11] Bradbury found that Negroes with superior qualifications to white incoming employees were hired at lower levels and were promoted at a markedly slower rate. This was true even when Bradbury took into account discrepancies in level of education at Negro colleges and matched 80 persons educated at comparable northern schools with superior qualifications for the Negro.[12]

Why then did the Negroes stay at their positions? Bradbury concluded that the lower rate of mobility out of the agency by Negroes represented proof of a general pattern of discrimination. The normal route for a non-promoted white of ability was to get advancement by transfer to another agency. Had as few as one-fifth of the federal agencies in Washington practiced truly equal employment, he argued, the discrepancy he found in treatment of equally capable workers could not have existed.[13]

---

[9] William Bradbury, Jr., "Racial Discrimination in the Federal Service" (Ph.D. dissertation, Columbia University, 1952; University Microfilms No. 4557).

[10] *Ibid.*, p. 71.

[11] Miller, *Rich Man, Poor Man*, p. 140.

[12] Bradbury, "Racial Discrimination in the Federal Service," Chapter 8, p. 89.

[13] *Ibid.*, p. 89.

As Bradbury's necessarily elaborate design, and indeed our own common sense, indicate, discrimination is not ascertainable merely through analysis of total employment figures. The number of Negro priests is the result of operative conditions quite distinct from the attitude of the church. Applicants with the necessary training and aspirations for such positions are by no means uniformly distributed throughout the various groups of our population. The most receptive personnel officer will have little success where there are—or even could be—no applications for the position.

III

The importance of governmental employment for the Negro community is reflected in the over-all statistics (*see* Table 4). From 1940 to 1962, 832,000 nonwhites found new employment in all levels of government—federal, state, and local. Of these new positions approximately 200,000 were filled at the federal level and approximately 600,000 at state and local levels. The early lag in the employment of Negroes at the local level is demonstrated by the fact that in 1940 when the national government was employing Negroes at a rate quite close to their proportion in the general population, approximately 10 percent, the employment of nonwhites by all governments was only 5.6 percent of total employment. In 1940 when only about one out of every four governmental employees was serving the federal government, about one-half of all nonwhites in governmental service were at the federal level. But by 1962 the proportion of nonwhites to total employment was almost the same at both the federal and the state and local levels.[14]

Table 4. Estimated Government Employment (Federal, State, and Local) in April of Selected Years*

Item	1940	1956	1960	1961	1962
Total number of government employees	3,845,000	6,919,000	8,014,000	8,150,000	8,647,000
Number of nonwhites employed in government	214,000	670,000	855,000	932,000	1,046,000
Nonwhites as a percentage of total	5.6	9.7	10.7	11.4	12.1

SOURCE: *The Economic Situation of Negroes in the U.S.*, U.S. Department of Labor Bulletin S-3, Revised 1962, p. 8.
*Figures cover all government services, including blue-collar work done directly by government agencies and teaching.

---

[14] *Ibid.*, and the Minority Group Annual Census of various dates.

An Analysis of Employment

Since World War II the percentage of nonwhite employment in the federal service has leveled off, with slight increases in actual number from year to year. The number of Negroes employed by the federal government has been, for several years now, greater by a small amount than the Negroes' representative share in federal employment.

At the local level the phenomenon of nonwhite employment has been given little attention, and no systematic evaluation of trends seems possible. As early as 1939 federal courts began to hold that discrimination in employment by state agencies violated the Fourteenth Amendment.[15] Nonetheless discrimination was remarkably pervasive both in {95} the North and the South. While all fifty states have provisions in their constitutions prohibiting discrimination in civil service on grounds of religion, only two (Michigan and Colorado) have also prohibited discrimination because of race. However, the passage of fair employment laws—which a majority of states now have—has usually led to less discriminatory practice on the part of the governmental authorities as well as those in private industry. The opportunities for expansion of Negro employment on the state and local levels over the past two decades have been even more significant perhaps than at the federal level, both in terms of absolute numbers, where the issue is clear, and in terms of the type of employment possible, which is more difficult to analyze.

Thus a study of Negroes in urban police forces in 1952 found that in nineteen major metropolitan areas Negro representation on the force ranged from 0.3 percent of the total to a high of 10.8 percent, while the proportion of Negroes in the population varied from 1.3 percent to 35 percent. In no case was the Negro representation as high as half the Negro proportion in the general population. In San Francisco the force employed only one-nineteenth the number of Negroes that their share in the population warranted, Dallas only one-sixteenth.[16] By 1960, 4 percent of firemen and policemen nationally were Negroes.[17] Raleigh, North Carolina, hired its first Negro fireman as late as February 15, 1963, although the police department had been employing Negroes for over twenty years.[18]

An investigation of the Michigan State Highway Department by the Michigan Fair Employment Practices Commission, on which a report was issued in March 1961, found that in general the agency had historically followed a policy of non-discrimination. This policy, however, had not been spelled out in any great detail, and after the passage of a state fair employ-

---

[15] Alfred Avins, "Weapons against Discrimination in Public Office," *Syracuse Law Review*, 14:24 (1962).

[16] William M. Kephart, "The Integration of Negroes into the Urban Police Farce," *Journal of Criminal Law and Criminology*, 45: 325-333 (1954).

[17] Miller, *Rich Man, Poor Man*, p. 90.

[18] *Crisis*, May 1963, p. 284. See also "The Negro Municipal Worker" (mimeographed report of the Richmond Urban League, September 1955).

ment law Negro employment in the agency spurted noticeably. The report also cited evidence of a "plateau beyond which Negroes have difficulty in advancing; it begins at supervisory levels?' It was further found that Negroes had less chance than whites of being hired and recruitment was somewhat biased against them. Finally, the {96} report concluded, community housing and public accommodation patterns influence not only the utilization of Negro personnel, but also a tendency of Negroes to exclude themselves from certain areas.[19]

So far as I can find, only Pennsylvania has published the results of a study of state agencies (1963). The pattern that emerges is instructive. The total number of Negro employees in state service is almost precisely proportionate to the Negro population, and therefore presumably is below the Negroes' share of the labor force in the state. Fully 87 percent of the employees working in state government at the time of the study were hired after 1955 when the state fair employment law was passed. Nevertheless the pattern of employment clearly reflected considerable discrimination in specific agencies. Three agencies employed no Negroes at all—in a state where 7.6 percent of the population is nonwhite—and less than 1 percent of the employees of three other agencies were Negroes. These included such structures as the Fish Commission, the Game Commission, and the State Police, Among the agencies with poor records was the Civil Service Commission itself. Of the 34 state departments, 25 employed fewer Negroes than the proportion of Negroes in the state would have warranted, Six agencies accounted for two-thirds of the Negro employees. Further, the Negroes were concentrated largely in clerical and sales and service positions. They constituted less than 2 percent of the unskilled workers and less than 1 percent of the skilled workers in state employment.[20]

Some of the indicated improvement in Negro employment by state and local government has undoubtedly resulted from the pressures of fair employment regulations. But improvement is evident even in states that have not passed such legislation. The growth at the local level has taken place apparently because of changing political and economic forces.

The drive for equal employment has shown there is potential for improvement even at the federal level at the present time. In five years, beginning in 1961, 26,000 new positions were filled by Negroes. There has been room for even more improvement at local levels, From 1961 to 1962 about 114,000 additional nonwhites were employed at all levels of government (see Table 4). The fact that state and local governments {97} have also moved toward employment of nonwhites at rates commensurate with the federal rate

---

[19] Louis Friedland, "Fair Employment Practices in the Public Service," *Public Personnel Review*, April 1962, pp. 109-113.

[20] *Survey of Non-White Employees in State Government* (Harrisburg: Pennsylvania Human Relations Commission, March 28, 1963).

An Analysis of Employment

would indicate that more is operative than sheer good will on the part of top administrators at the federal level. In short, a combination of economic and social forces has been working toward equalization of employment. As "better" jobs become available, and state and local services are viewed as less desirable, nonwhites move into those positions; as the political power of nonwhites increases, their ability to demand such job rights is augmented.

A pronounced lag exists in governmental employment of Negro women. The very high proportion of "wage board" and similar positions (see the next page for a summary of classifications) filled by Negro men at the federal level has helped boost total Negro employment in the service. Negro women have no such area of predominance but compete principally in the lower clerical positions. Negro women in 1980 constituted only about 11 percent of all employed women in the federal bureaucracy, a percentage point or two below the male proportion, though Negro women are much more likely to be in the job force than white women. (In 1965, 45 percent of Negro women were in the job force, compared with 37 percent of white women; in past years the difference was even greater.) Negroes constituted only 7 percent of all women employed in state and local public administration and 9 percent in educational services at a time when nonwhites as a whole constituted nearly 11 percent of all government employees. On a velocity basis, on the other hand, the gains by Negro women have been extremely impressive. In the decade between 1950 and 1960, the number engaged in state and local public administration more than doubled as did the number in the federal service. Governmental service including education loomed as the source of employment for nearly 10 percent of all Negro women in 1960, compared with only 7 percent a decade before.[21] Besides various school positions, government service provides ample opportunity in clerical and stenographic jobs. "If it were not for the Social Security people [as a source of employment] I don't know what we would do," a counselor at a Negro high school in Baltimore is quoted as saying.[22] In Washington, D.C., as in cities like Chicago, {98} Negro women are quickly and easily employed, partly as a consequence of a chronic clerical shortage. But the lower clerical positions share the attributes of laboring positions for men: they are dead-end positions, with little real opportunity for advancement and only nominal status and salary increases available as time goes on. These increases satisfy the need for minimal improvement. They just begin to emphasize the problem with regard to over-all advancement for 10 percent of our population, The problem of women in the federal bureaucracy is generally a special and complex one; the fact that Negro women disproportionately go

---

[21] *Negro Women Workers* in *1960* (Department *of* Labor Bulletin 287, 1963), especially pp. 44-45. Negro women generally earn closer to the average of white women than do Negro males in comparison with white males. *Miller, Rich Man, Poor Man*, pp. 91-98.

[22] "Report of the Social Security Administration on Personnel Practices" (mimeographed report, May 4, 1964), p. 18.

into the labor market adds to the general problem of status, advancement, and morale.

IV

In the federal service, the intermingling of racial with class and status problems is clearer than in most aspects of our society.

Class lines are rather neatly and decisively etched in the specification of pay plans. Under the Classification Act of 1949, as later amended, the bulk of the clerical, administrative, and professional positions in the government service are assigned to one of eighteen pay classes, representing an evaluation of the skill and responsibility required for the job. These classes range from GS 1, the simplest jobs, to CS 18. The classifications GS 16 to GS 18 were additions to the original scheme, first as an emergency measure to hold special personnel, such as scientists, but later integrated into the permanent system, They are referred to as "super-grades." About 45 percent of all government employees come under this system. The Post Office pay plan accounts for about 25 percent. Another 25 percent—predominantly in laboring and relatively low-skill jobs—are under a wage board arrangement, which attempts to adjust pay to prevailing market rates in the place of employment. (The remainder are in several small special pay plans.) Within these major divisions both class and status are carefully, even lovingly, demarcated.

It is likely that class and status considerations not only are more in evidence in government than in many if not most other bureaucratic structures, but also are more firmly and constantly implanted in the awareness of the participants. Status must be kept in evidence in governmental service for two major reasons. In the first place the stigmata create the distinction. In a democratic, bureaucratic structure, authority {99} is transmitted largely through the establishment of the hierarchy. In the second place the signs of station deliberately, legally, and necessarily are overt; a constitutional order except under extraordinary circumstances insists upon publicized conferral of offices and power. All who inquire can learn, and the entire bureaucracy is privy to the distinguishing characteristics, which include the validating criteria for rank.

At the same time, this awareness co-exists with great uncertainty. There is no external source of legitimation—property ownership, for example—for the status differential. In its purest sense the federal service is intended to be a meritocracy. Classification is presumably directly related to worth of individual services. It is at one and the same time an assessment of the individual's contribution and a creation of other individuals whose own authority and right to make the assessment is itself assessable and assailable. Prejudice, caprice, or error is the prerogative of authority which rests upon a nonrational or non-utilitarian base, but the appearance—or alleged appearance—of any of these is a source of conflict and doubt where prejudicial, capricious, or erroneous acts *ipso facto* indicate the lack of fitness for office of their perpetrators.

So while classification and pigeonholing create an insecurity among those permanently consigned to the lower depths of the bureaucracy, they also give rise to doubts at higher levels. The federal bureaucracy is nearly the embodiment of Riesman's other-directed America, replete with self-doubts, easily aroused. The pressures, however, are greatest at the bottom of the pyramid, where the right to question superiors does not fully compensate for the doubts raised about individual worth when classification purportedly is objective.

In any case, status and class, distinctions flow throughout the bureaucracy, in titles and designations, carpeting on the floor, distribution of flags, access to executive lunchrooms, and, not the least, pay. That these differentials are less than in industry does not alter the fact that they are actually more visible, less shielded from sight and consciousness, and more controversial than their analogues in private employment.

Because a sense of status and individual worth is a primary human need, increasing employment alone will hardly resolve the racial problem. The providing of jobs for the masses comes very close to {100} Irving Kristol's concept of "the remittance man."[23] In our society, the poverty-stricken are rarely left alone to starve. Rather, they are given some sort of compensation and excluded from numerous aspects of meaningful existence. Many feel that this is closely approximated in a good deal of government employment. Oddly, this attitude prevails even at upper regions of the bureaucracy. There is some feeling that make-work has been the pattern for establishment of a good many of the middle-level nonwhite positions throughout the federal service. Negroes all too often find that their newly created posts have no real duties. Often the accouterments of office are obviously beyond the level of work demanded. The Negro bureaucrat at the upper reaches is often given extra status, a fancier desk, than he would receive on the merits of his position. The suspicion that he is there to perform the function of Art Buchwald's Negro Ph.D. with an engineering background who speaks ten languages—to sit by the door to convince everyone of the egalitarian principles of the business office in which he is employed—haunts virtually every major Negro bureaucrat.

That there are some Negroes who are in a position to have this concern is evidence of the success of the equal employment program. On the whole, Negro leaders accept the strivings of the federal government with restrained approval. The approval must be given because of the facts: advances have been made; the restraint is due to the limited nature of the advances together with the lack of real cumulative programming for future advances.

Truly major changes have clearly occurred in the few years of the equal employment drive. Not only did Negroes garner some 28 percent of the

---

[23] *New Leader*, August 5, 1963, pp. 10-12.

increased positions in the federal service in the years 1961-1965, but the pattern of Negro employment within the service significantly altered. During those five years there was a decline of fully 5 percent in the proportion of Negroes who were under the wage board program and similar programs; this was accomplished through an actual small decline in such jobs and a heavy increase in the number of positions established under the Classification Act and in the appointive positions. Further, within the Classification Act categories, there has been a slight decline of Negroes at the GS 1 through 4 level, and an increase of 50 percent at the GS 5 through 11 level. From the GS 12 through 18 levels there has been almost a threefold increase. It is in the last two {101} categories that the most important progress presumably is taking place. If this can be the foundation for future development, then we may expect to see significant numbers of Negroes in positions of decision-making responsibility in the next decade. If, on the other hand, this represents merely an immediate concession with isolated, terminal advancement, then the prospect for the Negro's future rate of progress is clearly dismal. It is this uncertainty that accounts for part of the restraint in the approval the Negro community has given the governmental program.

Another important fact emerges from these same statistics: the Negro is still making slow progress in the higher decision-making echelons of the bureaucracy. The improvements that have occurred have hardly placed Negroes on a par with white bureaucrats in terms of distribution in positions of authority. Negroes still constitute only a little over 1 percent of all those occupying a GS 12 through 18 position, and only 3.4 percent of those at the 9 through 11 level, They still constitute 19 percent of all wage board employees and 82 percent of those who receive less than $5,000 under other pay plans.[24]

The change is thus relative to the initial differences. The measures taken to alleviate discrimination have in one sense been significant yet, compared with the pattern of differences still existing they may well warrant the description of tokenism. The spottiness of the record on a regional and agency basis also raises questions about the effectiveness of the program. Higher prestige agencies like the State and justice departments, as well as the Civil Service Commission itself—have generally had very modest improvements compared with less glamorous agencies like the Veterans Administration and the Post Office, which have seen more dramatic results. Differential rates also suggest a slowing down of progress and a declining zeal throughout the service.

It would be remiss, however, not to take into account the obvious differences in training and background at the present time possessed by the white and Negro communities. One does not overnight create a mass of individuals with requisite skills, training, and experience. As noted earlier in this discus-

---

[24] Derived from the Minority Group Annual Census of various dates, especially *Study of Minority Employment in the Federal Government* (Washington, D.C.: Government Printing Office, 1965).

sion, the mere announcement of intent to allow individuals to move without prejudice into positions of authority {102} is not sufficiently convincing to induce people to undertake the sacrifices entailed in entering upon necessary training and getting necessary experience. The willingness to delay gratification in the interest of greater future rewards, which is characteristic of middle-class society, is not characteristic of lower-class culture including most of the Negro culture. Changing the value system of Negroes to accommodate this pattern—which DuBois recognized in the early twentieth century as having importance second only to the Negroes' securing training and information[25]— is a difficult process which can be set in motion only after tangible signs that the delayed gratification will in fact result in greater rewards. Even at the present time it is not at all clear that accumulation of low-level skills by Negroes is as sure to be reflected in some economic advantage as highly advanced training is. Prejudice operates most insistently at the lower levels. Since it is easier to convince individuals to undertake low-level training, this lack of probability of reward is a serious deterrent to the general upgrading of the skills of the Negro community. Furthermore, the census data do not, at present at least, reflect improvements sufficient to induce new patterns. At every level of education the white profits from his educational experience more than his Negro counterpart; the disproportion grows greater, in short, as we move up the educational scale.[26] The fact is that older Negroes with even the best of college training are already largely bracketed into the positions that they will occupy the rest of their lives. Presumably the recent changes which have narrowed the educational gap between Negro and white males from 4 to 1½ years will be reflected in future data.[27]

But even if the inducements were more dramatically clear than they are, the situation could hardly change overnight. One does not change the total employment structure of a social group rapidly by inducing change in teenagers as they come onto the labor market. Even though the mass of youthful population will radically change the age composition of our society, and thus will effect dramatic "younging" of the society as a whole, the oldsters will still be with us, We do not have the option of wandering twenty years in the desert and letting the older {103} generation die off. A major student of ecology has concluded that "Whatever the future may hold with regard to the oncoming cohorts of young Negroes, the performance to date, together with the postulate that educational attainment is a background characteristic [for employment], enables us to make a most important prediction: the disparity between white and nonwhite levels of educational attainment in the general popula-

---

[25] W. E. B. DuBois, *The Training of Negroes for Social Power* (Atlanta University Leaflets, 1903), pp. 9-10. DuBois listed intelligence first, values second, the ballot third. See pp. 6-7.

[26] Miller, *Rich Man, Poor Man*, pp. 152-159.

[27] *Ibid.*, pp. 40-41.

tion can hardly disappear in less than three-quarters of a century. Even if Negroes now in their early teens were to begin immediately to match the educational attainment of white children, with this equalization persisting indefinitely, we should have to wait fifty years for the last of the cohorts manifesting race differentials to reach retirement age."[28]

Much the same problem exists in Israel where an older generation is actually even more divorced from Western culture, less inclined toward Western values of deferred gratification and technical know-how, than the American Negro. There, however, the status of the older generation as greenhorn immigrants and the institution of universal conscription with the concomitant opportunity for training on a broad social scale, lead to the inculcating of new values under dramatic circumstances. Within the Negro community, on the other hand, in spite of its current emphasis upon new and youthful leaders, there is a much more definite survival of older cultural values.

V

We have been discussing the federal service as though it were a monolithic structure. But in many respects it is not, and we will analyze the departments and agencies one by one in a subsequent chapter. In addition, the problem of overcoming discrimination in federal employment is not merely nationwide but varies from region to region. The area in which the solutions are the simplest and in which the greatest progress has been made is the District of Columbia. Here the national government utilizes Negro employees in part because the Negro community is the largest available source of labor. To some extent the District of Columbia is a southern city. (One is reminded of President {104} Kennedy's characterization of Washington as combining southern efficiency and northern charm.) In the District, however, the importance of the federal government as the major employer has resulted in the gap between white and Negro income being only about as great as that in the more heavily unionized—and therefore more seniority conscious and more regularized—urban North. At the same time it must be noted that the statistics on income in the District of Columbia exclude the suburbs which are "outstate"; the higher-level bureaucrats live in these suburbs and therefore the income figures for whites in the District are misleading.[29]

The discrepancy between central headquarters and the regions in the employment of Negroes is striking. Negroes constituted in 1965 nearly one in four employees in the Washington metropolitan area, but only about one in

---

[28] Otis Dudley Duncan, "Population Trends, Mobility and Social Change," paper prepared for the Seminar on Dimensions of American Society, Committee on Social Studies, American Association of Colleges for Teacher Education, p. 52. Quoted in Arnold Rose, *Assuring Freedom to the Free* (Detroit: Wayne State University Press, 1965), pp. 129-130.

[29] Miller, *Rich Man, Poor Man*, pp. 85-86.

eight throughout the federal service. One in five Negro employees is employed in Washington, while only about one in eight or nine of all employees is so located. The difference in distribution by classification is similar. Thus nearly 1,100 Negroes are employed at GS 12 to 18 levels in Washington out of 2,800 in the total federal service; i.e., nearly 40 percent are in the metropolitan area. Similarly 27 percent of all Negroes at GS 9 to 11 levels are so employed. (This picture is modified, however, by the relatively greater number of Negroes in wage board positions in the District of Columbia than elsewhere and by a somewhat less concentrated situation in the postal field services.) As one moves away from the core into the periphery of the federal service one finds sharp variation based on local custom, with the obvious result that the Negro is sadly disadvantaged in the Deep South. Alabama with its roughly 30 percent Negro population has 60,000 federal employees of whom only about 11 percent are Negro. Mississippi with almost a 40 percent Negro population has 16,000 federal employees of whom only about 9 percent are Negro—this, however, represents a dramatic 450 percent increase over the situation in 1964, when the first regional census began to be published.[30]

In 1965 Leroy Collins, the former governor of Florida, then head of the Community Relations Service, and later Undersecretary of Commerce, criticized sharply the rate of progress at the regional and local levels in changing the pattern of discriminatory hiring by federal {105} agencies. President Johnson cooperated fully in the publicity given to such criticism and reiterated his strong intention of eliminating discrimination wherever it might exist.[31] With the beginning of publication in 1964 of reports on Negro employment, not only agency by agency, but also by civil service region and by states and standard metropolitan statistical areas, bases for analyzing population distribution and geographic progress became available. In short, emphasis has shifted from broad national data, which often obscure the real sources of the problem, to local data which permit pinpointing of issues.

---

[30] "Study of Minority Employment," 1965.

[31] *New York Times*, March 26, 1965, p. 23.

6
The Machinery of Equality

I

{106}
AMERICANS have been more prone to tinker with the machinery of government than to try to understand it. Conservative spokesmen who emphasize the "recalcitrance of the human material" of policy and ultra-liberals like the spokesmen for the Freedom Democratic party in Mississippi who prattle about vague and undefined "social revolutions" share a lack of concern with day-to-day institutionalization of policy.[1] Indeed at least for the latter group institutionalization would basically be regarded as the burial of true concern for individuality.

Yet the history of the search for equal employment in governmental service is clearly the history of developing machinery. Though there has repeatedly been individual action that burst through the previous modes and bounds of institutional behavior, there have also been numerous examples that demonstrate the limitations of individual action. To strengthen the resolve of those who are concerned about civil rights, to remind those who would forget their responsibilities, has in fact been much more of a necessity than to convert people to new philosophies.

Theoretically, after all, equal employment has always been the policy of the federal government, at least since the Pendleton Act. The problem {107} has been to implement it. All the recent flurry of presidential and congressional action, the changes in administrative structure and accounting procedure—all these represent the culmination of a quarter century of effort to define fully and finally the content of that policy and the manner in which it is to be enforced. The machinery embodies the idea, and governmental structure (at least in its embryonic and developing stages), the evolution of policy as it seeks to assert its logical consequence.

As A. F. Bentley points out, the political structure is itself a physical manifestation of group conflict, an index of social pressures generated by competing interests.[2] New structures, new policies collide with the old, representing the congealing and resolution of past struggles; thus, new equilibria are

---

[1] See, for example, Norm Fruchter, "Notes on SNCC," *Studies on the Left*, 5: 74-80 (1965).

[2] A. F. Bentley, *The Process of Government* (Bloomington, Ind.: Principia Press, 1949).

reached sometimes with relative finality, other times with a continuous and protracted tension, leading to new solutions.

The pace of the civil rights movement has been so rapid and the demands made by the Negroes so far-reaching and varied that there has been no tendency for them to become overly enamored of any specific administrative device. Nor has any structure fully and completely satisfied civil rights advocates. Indeed there has been remarkable and rapid structural transformation—in many directions—reflecting the turbulent ebb and flow of power and policy in the whole area of civil rights.

Even the strongest of the "principles" invoked have later been decisively revised, with little notice or discussion. Since the time of the first Committee on Fair Employment Practice it had been almost an article of faith that "...the Civil Service Commission is not properly the main enforcement agency of a permanent federal non-discrimination policy. The purpose or function of this agency is not properly related to the work of changing discrimination which is an integral part of our social system and our everyday behavior. It cannot police discrimination in the federal service without introducing such rigidities into its rules and regulations as to impair its function as a central personnel agency."[3] Thus the argument was that only an independent agency could enforce equal employment. Roosevelt, Truman, Eisenhower, {108} and Kennedy all accepted this reasoning and Johnson as Vice President as well as in his first two years as President played so decisive a role in shaping the President's Committee on Equal Employment Opportunity that it was assumed this structure would be a fixture. Yet the entire arrangement was set aside and responsibility for the program entrusted to the regular administrative structures—i.e., principal operating responsibility was given to the Civil Service Commission, which was entrusted with supervising the regular departments, with some rather indeterminate allocation of responsibility to the Labor Department as well. While this action betokened the President's confidence in the interest in the anti-discrimination program of John Macy, not only the Civil Service Commission administrator but also a special adviser to the. President, it meant that specialized groups outside regular channels would be afforded less opportunity to exert external pressure on the bureaucracy.

It is probable that President Johnson's decision to abolish the committee and his newly founded Council on Equal Opportunity will have few immediate policy effects, for as we have seen the tendency of the program of the past few years has been centrifugal, with a profusion of organizations involved in the program. The President's committee indeed encouraged this sort of development. The committee regarded itself more as a catalyst than as an implementer of the program. Executive Order 10925 placed the responsibility upon

---

[3] John A. Davis, "Nondiscrimination in the Federal Agencies," *Annals of the American Academy of Political and Social Science*, 244: 74 (March 1946).

each agency for implementation, rather than upon the committee alone. The committee itself had a tiny budget and staff that under no conditions could effectively police the federal bureaucracy; the emphasis had to be—even more than would be usual in so involuted an organization—on persuasion in the securing of largely voluntary compliance. The reliance on persuasion was in accordance with Johnson's preferred method of operation, just as the small budget reflected his genuine enthusiasm for penny-pinching. Furthermore, the committee thereby was almost immunized from certain lines of attack. Successes could be attributed to its effective use of persuasion, such results on a small budget being particularly deserving of self-congratulation; failures could be assigned to the agency, where, after all, implementation of the program was supposed to take place.

Therefore, activity at the departmental or agency level has been the key to progress in equal employment opportunity; the extent and {109} character of that activity reflect the differential zeal of the top administrators and the degree of their control over the agency. Some—Veterans Administration, Labor, Commerce—have their own procedures at least as elaborate as those of the committee had been. Monthly statistics, for example, are accumulated in most departments, and administrators are constantly reminded about the program.

The continued use of employment opportunity officers who are separate from personnel officers is among the more interesting aspects of the program. The idea behind the separation of function, as indicated earlier, is that complaints should not be funneled through those persons responsible for the initial policy. Otherwise judges would be judging their own previous actions. The President's committee was authorized under Executive Order 10925 to make exceptions to this pattern and some agencies do in fact place responsibility for employment policy on the personnel office. The Post Office for example has combined personnel and the employment policy lines, except for investigative purposes. In compensation, the Post Office has an elaborate hearing procedure in which officers whose normal duties run the gamut of departmental functions are also trained as employment policy inspectors. They hear complaints at installations other than their own so as to minimize the possibility of bias, In other agencies the commanding officer or chief supervisor may be the official employment policy officer while some staff member performs the *de facto* functions, The Navy follows this procedure, which in effect makes equal employment a command function. At least one prominent figure in the employment policy field—the former executive director of the President's committee—believes that this has been a successful procedure in that it reduces the visibility of the employment officer and shields him from political criticism. In other agencies, particularly those of middling size, the carrying out of employment policy is assigned to a staff assistant or special assistant to the chief administrator as part of miscellaneous duties. In the State Department during the time the employment policy officer was G. Mennen Williams. His responsibility as Assistant Secretary for

African Affairs took precedence over his administrative functions. Richard T. Fox, for several years designated neither as employment policy officer nor as a personnel employee, handled many of the chores that would normally be handled by the equal employment officer.

{110} The use of an annual visual census or "head count" of Negro employees as the method for determining compliance with the executive order was agreed upon at a White House conference in 1955. The need to make such a count resulted from abolishment of racial classifications on employee records in most agencies of the bureaucracy after World War II. Since 1961 the census figures have been available for public review. Before that time they were confidential.

The obvious—and frequently heard—comment is that proof of discrimination, or non-discrimination, cannot come from statistics. The needs of agencies vary so much that results are misleading. Thus the record of the National Aeronautics and Space Administration is relatively poor because of its need for many highly trained aeronautical engineers, while the Post Office looks good because of the preponderance of relatively unskilled labor that it needs. Conceding some of the force of this argument, the committee asserted that even though statistics do not give answers they do provide a basis for asking pertinent questions.

The unusual head count arrangement—administrators annually attempted to identify the racial background of members of their staff, sometimes by guessing—was itself a subject of some controversy. The desire to have a progress report on Negro employment conflicted with the fear that racial notations in personnel folders might contribute to discrimination or (equally harmful) merely suggest the possibility of systematic prejudice by supervisors. As personnel officials exasperatedly complained, the, equal employment opportunity program asked them to keep accurate tabs on nonwhite employment, while insisting that no record be kept. The paradox was admitted and regretted. Spokesmen pointed out, however, the multiple objectives implicit in the program, noting that this policy represented a considered judgment that occasional inaccuracies and the tediousness of regular head counts were less serious costs to the program than the evils of racial classification on personnel records might be.

Late in 1965 Secretary of Labor Wirtz openly espoused restoration of racial classification on federal employment records to make achievement in minority employment subject to more precise calculation. In February 1966 the new regulations announced by John Macy included provision for agencies' compiling records of racial or national origin. These files were to be available for statistical purposes only and the {111} records of individual employees were not to be made available to supervisors. Criticism from NAACP leader Herbert Hill and Senator Sam Ervin of North Carolina followed the announcement. The new regulations, as implemented in the Department of Labor and the Post Office, made filling out information on race voluntary with the employee. Secretary Wirtz further announced that his department would not assemble records in states where such identification was illegal.[4]

Bearing in mind the discrepancies—usually small—inherent in the head count method (in at least one agency, however, there has been major disagreement between the employment policy officer and the office of personnel over the accuracy of the head count), and the problem now created by voluntary racial identification, with differing refusal rates in various agencies, we can use the data to pinpoint areas of Negro employment or the lack thereof. Agencies that have not shown improvement can be winnowed out from those who do. Sub-units of the same agency—particularly regional units having the same function as some other—can be compared and assessed. Like complaints, the census figures can function as the beginning of an inquiry into the total pattern of employment in an agency. As statistics pile up year after year, agency by agency, in gradually more refined form, that inquiry can become more and more informed.

The President's committee was not limited to investigation of complaints against an agency, for it had authority to "scrutinize and study employment practices." Thus, the head count was officially an instrument of positive policy, as is the voluntary census now. The independent role of, first, the President's committee and, now, the Civil Service Commission in auditing on the basis of complaints, and their power to take jurisdiction on their own initiative also have encouraged belief in the impartiality of the process. This has both stimulated the filing of complaints and encouraged the correction of abuses.

The administrative level of equal employment opportunity officer has varied considerably. In some agencies he is directly under the authority of the chief administrative official of the agency, in others he reports to an administrator two or three levels down. The amount of time he may have to devote to this function also varies considerably depending upon the establishment and the top administrators. Few {112} agencies have full-time employment officers. However, many agencies have a number of employees whatever their titles with intergroup functions. Clearly leading them all is the Defense Department; it has very involved problems of an intergroup nature in connection with contracts, community relations, and the military establishment, as well as intergroup problems with civilian employees. A large number of highly specialized persons are employed full time in dealing with these problems. The Veterans Administration has a small central staff, with a large-scale program for temporary use of other employees as need arises, as does the Post Office Department. (The latter two are generally credited with having the best developed equal employment programs in the government service.) In other agencies the function is merely a very minute portion of a position; the person holding it has many diverse activities and in effect limits his equal

---

[4] *New York Times*, October 29, 1965, p. 38; February 25, 1966, p. 17; June 4, 1966, p. 29.

employment activity strictly to the handling of complaints.

Regardless of the formal separation from personnel, equal employment opportunity officers vary in their actual day-to-day relations with that division. The employment opportunity officer, as noted above, may limit himself to hearing complaints and may simply view himself as a judge; if so he is very likely to keep himself aloof from the personnel office so as not to be influenced by it. If, on the other hand, he is particularly interested in recruitment or retraining, he may emphasize close liaison with the personnel division. Finally, the degree to which the equal employment opportunity officer feels a need to develop relationships with personnel officers may depend upon his confidence in their attitudes toward compliance with the executive orders; in the Veterans Administration, for example, the equal employment officers indicated they had little contact with personnel officers precisely because they had confidence in the program and in the accomplishments of the personnel office. They felt they could devote themselves to looking at the records of individual installations and to working at the local level. On the other hand, Internal Revenue, which historically has had a spotty equal employment record—very good in some regions, quite poor in others and which has been faced with the prospect of a cutback in its personnel in recent years, has seen fairly close relations, with the hiring of at least one former personnel man for full-time employment policy duties.

There is also considerable variation in what occupies an employment {113} opportunity officer's time. In general the committee and most officers have downgraded the complaint function. This is in accordance with the recommendations of the Eisenhower committee and the wording of President Kennedy's executive order. Some officers emphasize strongly the recruitment function and, particularly when they are Negroes, they may inject considerable vigor into the recruitment process. Another contribution may very well turn out to be simple placement of a small number of individuals; there is considerable evidence that a good deal of the effort of employment officers goes into such placement. Finally, the basic problem the officer is dealing with may be attacked in more long-range ways, through examination of agency practices and study of alternatives to these practices. The State Department, for example, has undertaken programs for evaluation of the Foreign Service officers examination and has aided a training program for potential Foreign Service officers held at Howard University. Similarly, the Social Security Administration has had a citizens committee make recommendations for future development.

Employment officers also vary in the extent to which they regard their decisions as determinative. Some expect immediate compliance with decisions, others seem to await battles and look to the appeal machinery for support. No doubt, all this depends in large measure on the degree of support that the officer gets from his superiors as well as upon the complexities of the problems that face him internally. Under Executive Order 10925 final decisions were to be made by the employment policy officer unless the matter was referred to the President's committee or, on his own initiative, the executive vice chairman of the committee assumed responsibility for the case. On the whole, the committee preferred to encourage resolution at the department level, making recommendations rather than giving orders.

The charge that the fair employment program has some of the aspects of a minority group WPA is not completely without merit. In agency after agency a major portion of the increase in positions of GS 14 or above held by minority group members has been in intergroup relations. This has resulted in an influx of Negroes in higher positions, as well as white intergroup counselors, many of whom are organized in the National Association for Inter-Group Relations (NAIRO), an active interracial group which has in turn recommended that intergroup specialists be hired throughout the government.

{114} The Civil Service Commission's reabsorption of equal employment functions, with the phasing out of the President's committee in 1966, was not a sudden process. Over the previous five years the commission took an ever increasing role in the equal employment program, consistent with its responsibilities for personnel. It specified promotion procedures, rewrote evaluation norms, emphasized equal employment in personnel handbooks and directives, as well as directly intervened in specific instances. The regularization of the program by establishing specified personnel procedures, including routine examinations and probing for irregularity, has increasingly been a task undertaken directly by the commission.

Through their responsibility to recruit for many positions in many departments, Civil Service Commission employees have been able to exercise wide influence. Civil Service administrator John Macy has personally seen to it that the commission is active in promoting equal employment; on occasion, particularly in the early years, he intervened directly, calling the attention of an agency director to specific situations, as when he pointed out to a fellow member of the Equal Employment Opportunity Committee, the Secretary of Health, Education, and Welfare, a discriminatory pattern in the Social Security Administration. Oddly, though, the commission as an employer of its own force—rather than as an overseer of the personnel policies of other agencies—has no great reputation in the Negro community. The statistical record of its own equal employment program is acknowledged by its top administrators to lack impressiveness and certainly would seem to be one of those that could stand improvement, even after some dramatic increases at high GS levels in 1965.

While the committee and the commission have concentrated on the overall statistical record of minority employment, two other foci of acknowledged political power, the Democratic National Committee and the White House staff, have been responsible for the dramatic and the attention-getting appointments.

At the level of position these units normally deal with—bureau chief and similar posts in Washington and major administrative positions such as postmasters or federal attorneys elsewhere—race becomes merely an additional factor in consideration of candidates in intense competition for what are regarded as desirable federal openings. Louis Martin of the National Committee has described his aim as one of {115} making "breakthroughs" which would have political advantage with minority group voters. The National Committee, for example, circulated a brochure listing Negro officeholders and emphasizing the President's role in equal employment.

The White House has not stopped at mere placement of Negroes into formal positions. Lee White on occasion circulated a memo to all agencies asking them to list not only all minority group members holding significant offices, but also the portion of their time devoted to efforts on behalf of minority groups—presumably to strike a blow at one of the major Negro complaints, that an inordinate number of minority group officeholders were solely concerned with the equal employment program itself.

II

The regional civil service agencies and the Civil Service Commission branch managers perform functions at the local level similar to those of the commission itself at the national level. They encourage the development of new procedures, supervise the collection of statistics, and evaluate and develop new techniques for recruitment. Community surveys have been conducted under the auspices of both the Civil Service Commission and the President's committee to evaluate all the work of federal organizations in a specific locale, and to point to areas of possible improvement.

In 1963, for instance, such a survey was made in Minneapolis under the auspices of the St. Louis Region, Civil Service Commission, by a team headed by Eugene Spika, St. Paul branch manager of the U.S. Civil Service Commission. (Mr. Spika is one of eleven Civil Service Commission employees honored for his work in implementing and encouraging equal employment opportunity in the federal service. The existence of such awards is an illustration of the prominence given by the commission to the equal employment program.) The team found no evidence of overt discrimination, pointing to the fact that the proportion of Negroes employed was higher than their share in the community population, but did find fault with the recruitment procedures of several agencies, and suggested changes. As a consequence the Post Office, which had actually been commended for its performance in the area, altered its employment policies so as to provide for Negroes among the top three applicants for a job a statement of reasons when they are {116} not hired. The report also found at least one instance—the Department of Justice agencies—where no Negroes were employed and where attitudes that were somewhat questionable were expressed by administrators. One of these agencies thought Negroes should probably not be utilized by it because of "cultural differences."[5]

The survey team found "a high correlation between the intensity and frequency of motivational actions by higher headquarters and the response of the various installation managers. Few have generated an aggressive program of their own volition." Passive acceptance of applicants was generally the attitude unless such external activation took place. Thus, the "Federal Aviation Agency, Minneapolis Office, could not be interested in the quest for affirmative action until its Regional Personnel Officer in August 1963 visited the area and attempted to contact all minority group leaders. He also established a policy that the local Federal Aviation Agency Coordinating Officer should become well acquainted with the Negro leaders. This action changed the Federal Aviation Agency picture overnight from a negative to a positive one."[6]

This survey also provided an interesting evaluation of the deputy employment policy officer. The team found that in some agencies (Corps of Engineers and Air Force) the deputy "is charged with (and is fulfilling) realistic responsibilities for measuring program effectiveness ... throughout the entire range of personnel management activities." In the Veterans Administration, however, "the delegation of the Deputy Employment Officer's responsibility is usually limited to investigations of specific complaints (in the nature of an *ad hoc* responsibility)." Even more significant are their comments about the deputy employment policy officer in smaller installations, which after all are rather typical of many throughout the country: "[He] is usually located at a higher echelon, and the main emphasis is on employees knowing the name and address of the Deputy Employment Policy Officer. In general, the Deputy Employment Policy Officer program is not accomplishing the intended results and there is skepticism both on the part of applicants and Negro community leaders that it is functioning as it should."[7]

The survey team was perhaps reflecting a general attitude on the part of civil service officers, who are often not friendly to the deputy employment officer concept, but nevertheless their criticism is not too wide of the mark. In many organizations the deputy employment officer is merely a letterhead name or a secondary title for an individual who is not truly concerned with that function.

The procedure under which the employment officers work is relatively similar from structure to structure. Each installation has a deputy employment officer, and an employee may complain directly to him, to the agency

---

[5] St. Louis Region, Civil Service Commission, "Report of Twin Cities Equal Opportunity Review" (mimeographed report, Minneapolis and St. Paul, March 13, 1964), pp. i-vii and 2-3.

[6] *Ibid.*, pp. 1 and 7.

[7] *Ibid.*, p. 2.

deputy employment officer in Washington, or to the Civil Service Commission (earlier the executive chairman of the President's committee). In the latter instances complaints are channeled back to the local or, as in the Post Office, the regional employment officer. The local deputy employment policy officer will then investigate the complaint, provided it is not obviously frivolous. The investigation also generally involves an attempt at informal conciliation, with the officer suggesting some solutions. If the complainant is not satisfied, he may request a formal hearing, at which he may be represented by counsel, cross-examine witnesses, and call witnesses to challenge the report of the investigator. A formal hearing officer is designated who keeps a record of the proceeding and transmits the record or a summary along with his recommendation to the agency employment opportunity officer in Washington for a final decision. If the complainant is not satisfied at this level he can appeal to the Civil Service Commission, which may make its own review. (Earlier the final appeal was to the executive vice chairman of the President's committee.) The hearing record is informal and the recommendations of the local employment officer are not necessarily fully available to the complainant. Legal fairness is required but not all the rigorous standards of courtroom procedure and due process are followed.

The major changes inaugurated by the Civil Service Commission in its initial statement of rules for its new responsibilities in equal employment seem well calculated to strengthen the program. Agencies are ordered to develop community programs on equal employment. Disposition of complaints must be reported to the commission, even in the absence of an appeal. Withdrawal of a complaint does not end the matter: an explanation of the withdrawal and a judgment by the hearing officer as to whether the complaint had merit are prescribed to minimize {118} pressure upon employees to withdraw complaints. The regulations make explicit the positive purposes of even the grievance procedure. The emphasis is upon programmatic elimination of discrimination, not simply upon alleviating an individual's sense of deprivation.

As a result of a complaint there may be a formal finding of discrimination, which does little except attach a clear-cut stigma to the situation. Or there may be a recommendation for "corrective" action; this does not necessarily mean that there was a finding of prejudice. Perhaps bad personnel policy is being followed or a sufficient case on other grounds is made out by the complainant. A remedial measure of intermediate severity is the ordering of a post-audit of promotions or other personnel policy in the unit. Occasionally correction may take the form of an ongoing audit over a period of time for employment and/or promotions. These latter are only rarely ordered and only when there is indication that questionable policies are in fact being followed.

The bulk of complaints are handled, for obvious reasons, at the informal conciliatory level. Administrators have no desire to appear to be dragging heels on the equal employment program. Often the matter at stake is a promotion involving only an upgrading in rank with no increase in responsi-

The Machinery of Equality

bilities, and this may be accomplished either through moving the person into a vacancy at the higher level or through some administrative restructuring including reclassification of his job with the consent of the Civil Service Commission. No central record is kept of informal complaints resolved in the field, but indications are that they make up the largest component of total complaints. This is evidenced even in the record on formal complaints. For example, the Veterans Administration processed 341 formal complaints from March 1961 through the end of 1964. In only 59 cases were formal hearings held, with corrective action taken in 29, or nearly half.[8]

For all its informality, the complaint procedure is a costly one on all sides. Considerable time and effort are required. The forms and records that must be kept, while not as voluminous as court records, are nonetheless usually more demanding of administrative effort than the specific problem would seem to warrant. From the standpoint of those interested in maintaining equal employment as a vigorous program complaints have an ambivalent character. On the one hand they are necessary {119} to call attention to problems. On the other hand, as one expert in the field observed, "Complaints have a tendency to eat you up." The time that must be devoted to the individual complaint is disproportionate to any possible results, if the complaint is viewed merely on its own merits. However, as noted earlier, complaints may serve as indices to problem areas, as indications of the nature of developing problems and the trends in different agencies toward meeting the situation. But complaints are not always a good index of what is happening in a department; they may be high in a division in which there are aggressive employees or administrators who take special care to acquaint employees with their rights and to assure them that complaints will not result in later disadvantages. Whitney Young has observed that, as a consequence, "far more benefit is derived from placing the laws on the books than from actual complaints and adjudicated cases. This is because there are very few actual complaints.... What has happened, however, is that when many of these FEPC regulations went into effect there were people who welcomed them because they wanted to take advantage of the skills of Negro workers.... The big shift comes when the laws are passed."[9]

From time to time federal employees have taken their cases to local and state commissions on civil rights, in addition to the President's committee. (Indeed, the "Report of the Twin Cities Equal Opportunity Review" criticized Negro leaders for a tendency to advise employees to appeal on each and every front.[10]) An extreme example involved a complex case at the Minneapolis Veterans Administration Data Processing Center in 1964 and 1965, which was

---

[8] Letter to Malcolm Feeley by Blake Turner, Veterans Administration, February 17, 1985.

[9] Whitney M. Young, Jr., *To Be Equal* (New York: McGraw-Hill, 1964), p. 46.

[10] "Report of Twin Cities Equal Opportunity Review," pp. vii and 43.

vigorously pursued by Seth Phillips, executive secretary of the St. Paul Human and Civil Rights Commission. This for a time was the only instance in which an employee who had gone through the equal employment procedure then appealed to a federal district court. No ruling ever resulted, for the complainant received a promotion and eventually withdrew his suit.

This state-federal overlap has not always contributed to a happy relationship and, as a matter of fact, state civil rights commissioners tend on the whole to be critical of the federal equal employment program. Probably the leading critic is Carl Glatt, formerly of the Kansas Commission on Civil Rights, later with the West Virginia Human {120} Rights Commission, who has openly criticized the federal program. As he has explained, "We remain critical of a federal agency investigating itself—there is a natural tendency for self-exoneration. . . . Mostly the federal agencies have been upheld by their internal appeals procedures." Mr. Glatt also found investigators, generally, but particularly those supervising compliance efforts of federal contractors, "untrained and at times unsympathetic for civil rights. They tend to find No Probable Cause when a more thorough investigation would have proven discrimination. This has been embarrassing to the Kansas Commission on Civil Rights to be processing a case on a Probable Cause only to have the respondent employer cite the exonerating No Probable Cause of the federal agency."[11] However, Mr. Glatt noted that recently—he made his comments in 1965—there seem to have been some improvements, although he was not sure whether this might not have been chance experience with particular teams of investigators. Mr. Phillips in an interview that same year reported similar experiences with untrained investigators at the local level. He suggested it was embarrassing that Minnesota standards, which he and Herbert Hill have characterized as among the weakest of all fair employment practices statutes in the country, have in fact proved more stringent than those applied by federal officers.

The suggestion of Mr. Glatt that investigators are often untrained is on the whole confirmed by experience. With the exception of the Post Office plan, no very extensive program for the training of investigators has been carried out by agencies, and as a result persons with relatively little experience and understanding are engaged as investigators or hearing officers at the local level. This, in turn, creates problems, for without a reasonably good hearing and record it is difficult for reviewers at higher levels to do their job adequately. The rather small number of complaints that are filed at any installation makes it extremely difficult to operate well-developed programs in each agency. Centralized hearing officers would have obvious advantages in that considerably more training could be given to them. Thus the Civil Service

---

[11] Letter to Malcolm Feeley by Carl Glatt, June 16, 1965. Some years after original publication of this book, Seth Phillips indicated to me at a public meeting he had misunderstood the situation he had complained about, and now thought the Federal action was justified.

The Machinery of Equality

Commission could, quite logically, take over this function in the interests of improving the quality of the hearing process. On the other hand, some of the advantages of informality and local responsibility which the present structure has might well be lost.

{121} It will be extremely interesting to see to what extent the Civil Service Commission abandons some of the practices of the past, striking out in new directions in the equal employment program. The President's September 1965 order transferring the program to the Civil Service Commission is distinguished by the relative brevity of his instructions and, compared with past executive orders, by much less specificity as to procedures and arrangements. This suggests that a new departure is envisaged in which some of the older shibboleths which have constituted the guidelines for the program for twenty years will be modified. The commission has wide scope and opportunity for experimentation. At least two of the more knowledgeable people in the equal employment opportunity area—John Feild and Harold Fleming—indicated in interviews with me in 1963 and 1964 their conclusion that the separate equal employment program has costs that probably outweigh its advantages, and that implementation of new programs is perhaps not best carried out through a system of deputy employment officers. Work on new programs could be done more directly if it were assimilated into the normal functions of those in charge of personnel, such as the Civil Service Commission and the regular personnel officers. Certainly those agencies that have been most successful have been at least as likely to have had integrated personnel functions as to have had the separate deputy employment policy officer arrangement. In addition it is clear that after a period of time the deputy equal employment opportunity officer becomes even more protective of the record of his agency than rank-and-file personnel officers. Personnel after all has many functions in which employment policy is only one. Personnel officers can admit to some failures in this area without jeopardizing their position. The deputy employment officer has unique vested interests. The obvious tack is for him to complain in the first year or two about how awful the situation is, and thereafter to indicate how fine matters have become since his advent.

Through its vigor and originality the Civil Service Commission seems to have regained effective control over the equal employment function. It is to be hoped that the commission will exercise that same creativity in streamlining the machinery of the past while retaining those aspects of the program which have proved valuable. If it is true that the program is successful primarily insofar as initiative comes from the top, with constant reminders to the agencies of the need for activity, then {122} such initiative must be instituted in a manner that does not destroy originality and drive. The opportunity for regularizing machinery and day-to-day dealings with the agencies is peculiarly and constantly available to the commission.

Its technical and administrative skill, and its resources—vastly greater than those which could reasonably be allocated to any single-purpose organization—are already evident in the rigor of the commission's new rules and in the implementation of more routinized review of the commission's new rules and in the implementation of more routinized review of agency actions. But its historic reputation for discrimination, compounded by an indifferent record in equal employment in recent years, breeds skepticism throughout the Negro community. Only an aggressive effort, with results evident within the ranks of the commission itself, can overcome this heritage of suspicion.

7

The Problem in the Departments: Some Illustrations

I

{123}
THE quest for equal employment is quite clearly not simply a drive for additional numbers, or for an improvement in the percentages. Indeed sometimes there is a strategic refusal of temporary improvements in numbers of Negroes employed, and even occasional acceptance of losses. During World War II a major agency offered to create a totally segregated unit of 10,000 with Negroes in administrative positions to an unprecedented degree and at unprecedented levels. The sponsors of the plan were perplexed when Negro leaders unanimously turned down the opportunity; they went away convinced that the Negroes were agitators who sought no true solutions but only trouble.[1] Again, desegregation in the border states has generally led to displacement of Negro teachers and drastic reductions in numbers of Negro principals and other administrators, often with substandard skills, who had been countenanced as long as they worked exclusively with the Negro community.[2] These are costs in seeking equality, costs which have not been seriously questioned and which the Negro leadership has been willing to pay.

{124} Advantages too must be carefully calculated and come in different varieties. To be sure, numbers are sought, but level of appointment is also a significant target. Like all prodigals, agencies where there has been no previous Negro service loom as more significant than others where appointment is a regularized matter. Also, some agencies have special prestige, status, and symbolic value. Some positions, of course, have policy implications for civil rights and the welfare of the Negro community—indeed for the equal employment program itself. Other positions have policy implications of a more general nature, and Negroes, like other citizens, wish to participate in general policy development.

Following Richard Hofstadter, we may classify the goals of political activity as follows: (1) goods and positions—the traditional loaves and fishes of

---

[1] William Bradbury, Jr., "Racial Discrimination in the Federal Service" (Ph.D. dissertation, Columbia University, 1952; University Microfilms No. 4557).

[2] U.S. Commission on Civil Rights, *Public Education* (staff report, 1963), p. 34. Cf. *New York Times*, October 14, 1956, p. 1.

partisan advantage; (2) values—ideology and policy considerations, the traditional programmatic aims of politics; (3) status—the symbolic recognition of a group's standing and importance, as in St. Patrick's Day proclamations or in the selection of a clergyman of one faith or another to deliver the invocation in a program.[3] James Q. Wilson has brilliantly argued the undesirability of the recent emphasis upon "amateur politicians" who pursue ideological programs and receive their primary rewards in the social interchange of political activity—"fun can be politics."[4] They contribute, he suggests, to political dogmatism, to a lack of practical flexibility in policies. Generally fears of this sort with regard to the civil rights movement are not of major significance. It is clear that the movement permanently and obviously is in quest of all the goals Hofstadter lists; for all the emotional and ideological centrality of the idea of equality, the effort always has had behind it the motive force of unemployment and material deprivation in the Negro community.[5] The objectives of the movement in seeking {125} equal employment in the federal service are also concrete and definite though diverse. And quite diverse structures and agencies can in turn meet each of these discrete goals.

In terms of numbers alone, only a handful of organizations have important potential. To an amazing degree the federal service is concentrated numerically in a few complex structures. Neither employment nor expenditures are divided equally among the nominally "major" units. Nor is departmental status, or any other label, even a rough indication of—one might almost say any clue at all to—size or fiscal resources. The labels attached to agencies are largely historical accidents. The Defense Department is, of course, the behemoth of them all, even if military personnel are excluded. Its civilian employees constitute 40 percent of all federal employees covered by the equal employment program. If one adds the employees of the Post Office (25 percent of the total) and the Veterans Administration (5 percent), 7 of every 10 federal civilian employees are accounted for. The departments of

---

[3] Richard Hofstadter, "The Pseudo-Conservative Revolt," in Daniel Bell, editor, *The New American Right* (New York: Criterion, 1955).

[4] James Q. Wilson, *The Amateur Democrat: Club Politics in Three Cities* (Chicago: University of Chicago Press, 1962).

[5] It is interesting to note that the civil rights movement continues to *use* the slogans "freedom" and "freedom now" as well as other variants on that theme, rather than the symbol of equality in its emotional chants. This is in conscious imitation of the slogans of African nationalist movements, especially of Nkrumah's party in Ghana. The invocation of such slogans thus provides a link to African independence and, in the eyes of the participants, adds a sense of dignity and brings into the situation a foreign policy aspect by publicly asserting a link between Negro "oppression" and "imperialist" white behavior in other parts of the world—a parallel which radical members of the civil rights movement seem to take seriously. The cry is also simple, direct, and therefore evocative. But it also illustrates the strong sense of instrumental use of ideology in the movement. Analogously, except for a very small core of devoted followers of Martin Luther King, "passive resistance" is not a matter of commitment but clearly one of tactics.

Health, Education, and Welfare, Agriculture, and Treasury employ another 10 percent, leaving only about 20 percent of federal employment in all agencies outside these six.[6]

The largest supply of new workers to meet federal manpower needs—and in the District of Columbia virtually the only such supply—is to be found in the Negro community. White employees come at a premium in terms of salary, rapid promotions needed to meet competitive offers, extra costs of recruitment in the field if they are to be brought from outside the District, and similar additional financial requirements. Increasingly agencies with a need for large numbers of employees turn to Negroes for natural reasons of economy and efficiency, the law of supply and demand being more significant here than the Civil Rights Act of 1964. A major appeal in recruitment is desirability of working conditions; thus equal employment programs are a virtual necessity for large-scale Negro recruitment and certainly an administrative efficiency, which can be shown to have dollars and cents advantages. The Veterans Administration, which formerly had the image of being a {126} "southern" agency and which badly needed to attract applicants for posts generally eschewed in our society, has been the bellwether agency of the federal government, and has achieved perhaps more than any other organization in the field of racial equality. This is not to deny the sincerity of those who initiated and carried out the reorientation, but simply to indicate that it was highly advantageous for the agency.[7]

While numbers are significant to the Negro community, particularly of course in times of general low employment (although its members experience almost permanent job depression), it has for years demanded as new symbols of achievement of equality higher posts in larger numbers. As the bureaucracy has expanded, the means of appearing to satisfy this demand without real accommodation—a Stephen Mead approach to racial equality—has become available. The tradition, at least as old as the New Deal days, exists of appointing Negroes to high positions to deal with other Negroes—federal employees or clientele groups. Somewhat glamorized social workers can be appointed in personnel offices to deal with the program of equal opportunity; the statistics will then show an improvement in Negro employment. Understandably, civil rights leaders have been making a conscious effort to obtain for Negroes positions that are in fact posts of discretion, that constitute genuine advances in achievement and steppingstones for future advantages as well. It must be added that generally the advent of a Negro, in whatever position, into an agency does constitute an advance; the first step is often the

---

[6] *Study of Minority Group Employment in the Federal Government* (Washington, D.C.: Government Printing Office, 1965).

[7] Bradbury, "Racial Discrimination in the Federal Service," pp. 174-176 and 439ff, points out that discrimination occurs when an organization has a choice of labor sources in the market place and that choice is compatible with other organizational goals.

hardest, and even the token positions often lead to further advances.

Recognition that some posts have significant policy implications for the civil rights movement and the Negro community generally has not necessarily always resulted in a push for large-scale Negro representation in decision-making, particularly in such areas as legal enforcement in the South. Careful calculation of advantages and disadvantages in seeking to obtain Negro representation must be made in such areas, for the acceptance of the entire program of civil rights can be affected. The goal of participation by Negroes at all levels of employment can temporarily be satisfied by their exerting outside pressure on white decision-takers; the latter, for a time, may be more effective legitimizers {127} of the program. Such a state of affairs can never be finally acceptable of course to civil rights advocates, though they may settle for it in an immediate situation.[8] Ultimately Negroes must and do expect to be represented throughout the Department of Justice, in the courts, in the Community Relations Service, and on law-enforcement agencies as their numbers and talents dictate.

In other areas where Negroes are among the principal clientele groups—welfare, housing, urban affairs—Negro representation is evident at upper decision levels, and Negro political power is flexed and recognized, much as that of other political groups. A clear exception has been the Department of Agriculture, where the political impotence of the southern rural Negro—the only significant body of rural Negro population in the country—is reflected in a traditional lack of Negro influence. Recent efforts to end this have not been so vigorous as to prevent the department's coming under attack by the Civil Rights Commission and by the Negro community.[9]

The more prestigious departments—State, Treasury, Justice itself—have seen less dramatic infusion of Negro personnel than many others. In part this reflects their vigorous standards in skills, information level, and experience. In part, too, these structures are largely insulated from some of the effects of presidential orders, and they comply with slightly less alacrity than more vulnerable and less venerable institutions. Similarly, congressional and executive "pets" are typically less compliant than the average agency. Interestingly, executive staff agencies—like the Bureau of the Budget and even, as we have already noted, the Civil Service Commission itself—typically do not have outstanding records in Negro employment.

---

[8] One of the great hallmarks of maturity of the civil rights movement was the displacement on television and in other mass media of liberal white sympathizers by the Negro leaders themselves as spokesmen for equal rights. This development, which occurred sometime in the late 1950's, has not so far as I can learn been noticed or commented upon and did not take place consciously or as the result of any predetermined policy.

[9] U.S. Commission on Civil Rights, *Equal Opportunity in Farm Programs* (Washington, D.C.: Government Printing Office, March 1965).

The Problem in the Departments

II

Behemoth: The Department of Defense. The current importance of the Department of Defense in the economy of the United States cannot be easily exaggerated. Its power as a direct employer and utilizer of {128} services as well as directly in the implementation of programs is that of the monopsonist. In the field of racial relations the department has many and diverse potentialities. In the armed forces it is a prime utilizer of Negro manpower and controls very closely the social relationships under which Negro servicemen function from day to day. In the ecological settings of its military installations, it can affect the racial patterns of community life. It is also, as we have seen, the largest single employer of civilians in the United States. Finally, as the nation's largest buyer, it exerts extraordinary influence. It has the power of life and death economically over some of the major industries in the country, and its influence is great with virtually all the major corporations whether they have direct military connections or not.

The tremendous importance of the department as a buyer, with the potential leverage that this gives in the securing of contract compliance on racial matters, is of all these the most clearly evident. It is unmistakable that if the government is to have an influence on industry in the field of equal employment through its purchasing power, it will primarily be through the Department of Defense. For this reason and probably also because of the temptation to put the burden for new programs and their dislocations on other shoulders than one's own, the Department of Defense has been more vigorous and aggressive in its contract compliance program than in its various "in-house" programs. This is not to say that it has been noticeably laggard in any direction, but it has assigned the greatest proportion of its available staff to the contract compliance area. On the whole, this would be regarded by most observers, both within and without the civil rights movement, as the most intelligent utilization of resources.

Before 1961 there was no department-wide program for equal employment. At that time "in-house" and contract compliance programs were coordinated by Norman Paul, Assistant Secretary for Manpower, and Ralph Horton was appointed director of the department's equal opportunity program. Each of the military services continued to provide its own administrative machinery. Paul and Horton were given coordinating powers in 1963, thus tightening the centralized control.

The services have tended to move in rather different directions. While the Army and Air Force have followed standard practice, in the Department of the Navy the equal employment function is a command function, exercised by the commanding officer. Many of the close observers {129} of the equal employment program had come to accept this as a not undesirable pattern well before the 1966 rules of the Civil Service Commission relaxed the pattern formerly set by the President's committee.

In manpower the Department of Defense has had a particular problem.

Many of its positions have been lower-middle-grade laboring jobs and the thrust toward modernization and super-efficiency which was part of the "McNamara-izing" of the Defense establishment involved the elimination of many blue-collar jobs. Thus at the same time that the pressure was on to increase Negro employment, structural and economic changes were taking place that worked in the opposite direction. The department has had to run very hard to stand still. At the higher levels, the department has done well, exceeding the other leading departments in its record, but it employs a smaller proportion of Negroes than the federal bureaucracy as a whole, and the further elimination of blue-collar workers continues to erode its over-all percentage.

The infusion of Negroes into the department has been most successful in the Secretary's own office. This reflects a tendency for newer agencies—the department is a postwar creation and McNamara has shaken it up drastically since 1961—to be able to comply with equal employment directives with greater ease than older agencies and to be more directly and firmly under the control of the central administrators.

The Navy, prominently known for its past practices of segregation, has been watched closely. For political reasons it has been extremely vulnerable, and it is, therefore, perhaps not surprising to note that its record of compliance is by far the best among the armed forces. Because of shipyard problems, it had to release a large percentage of Negroes in the lowest blue-collar positions but it managed to increase the number of Negro employees in the highest-paying blue-collar positions.

The Air Force, which as a newer agency might be expected to have fewer obstacles to equal employment, is probably less free of personal prejudice among administrators than most agencies and has notably lagged behind. While it has an average proportion of Negroes in GS 12-18 positions, its overall percentages are low. The Air Force has been relatively immune from political pressure and as a favorite of Congress has been able to pursue a largely independent course in its personnel policy. Its technical needs are of course high. In the view of outside {130} experts, as well as civil rights advocates, it has not developed a vigorous recruitment program, although its arrangements are not inherently prejudiced.

In the past few years the department has seriously re-examined its entire performance in equal employment, hiring the Potomac Institute as a contractor to make recommendations both for the contract compliance program and for the "in-house" programs. However, the Subcommittee on Manpower Utilization of the Committee on Post Office and Civil Service in the House of Representatives investigated the use of this contractor and its qualifications in official hearings. There are some indications both in the printed hearings and in the accounts of observers that the congressional investigation may have been instigated or carried on with the cooperation of the personnel officers in the Department of Defense who are unhappy about the jumping of channels in the equal employment program.[10] The department has as yet not revealed any over-all new patterns in equal employment resulting from the investigation.

Building a New Image: The Veterans Administration and the Patent Office. Although the Veterans Administration has traditionally been regarded as one of the agencies least receptive to the Negro, in the postwar era it has exerted itself to change that image to such effect that it won an accolade from *Ebony* as "the government's most integrated agency."[11] With about one-quarter of its employees Negro, the Veterans Administration has had good reason to seek a better image among minority group employees. The agency has emphasized equal employment opportunity positively through a series of bulletins, memos, and discussions on equal employment—not just the infrequent one or two—and has sought the type of publicity represented by the *Ebony* article, to the point of arranging to reprint and distribute such tributes. It has conspicuously rewarded Negro administrators and has consciously sought top-grade Negro talent and entrusted them with responsibility at the very highest level of administration. Pictures of Negroes and whites jointly at work, or in conference, as well as of Negroes in technical and professional roles are very commonly distributed {131} throughout the department, and Negro colleges are a favorite target of Veterans Administration recruiters.

The departmental machinery for complaints is relatively centralized and aggressive. On one occasion the Veterans Administration sought an order from the President's committee requiring the Civil Service Commission to take corrective action against a discriminating supervisor by removing, not merely reprimanding, him. The President's committee felt it did not have the authority to order suspension of civil service rules, and so the matter ended. Nonetheless, it was an instance of aggressiveness on the part of the Veterans Administration which illustrates why it has been able to change its image from an agency unfriendly toward Negroes to "the government's most integrated agency."

Less successful in image-building has been the Patent Office. In the past the Patent Office was on more than one occasion called "the most racially-oriented agency in Washington." Basically it was a "southern" agency in tone and some of its present bad reputation is due to this past pattern. One recent assistant commissioner, Horace Fay, Jr., a patent attorney from the North, feeling that a good deal of the problem was simply a matter of poor human relations, spent quite a bit of his time on such mechanical "trifles" as inducing

---

[10] *Use of Contractors: Equal Opportunities in the Military Services*, Hearings before the Subcommittee on Manpower Utilization of Committee on Post Office and Civil Service, House of Representatives, Eighty-Eighth Congress, First Session, November 5, 1962 (Washington, D.C.: Government Printing Office, 1963).

[11] *Equal Employment Opportunity in the USVA* (pamphlet, undated).

the professional staff and supervisors to say "hello" to other employees as they walked through the halls. An agency of some 2,500 employees of whom one-half are professionals, the Patent Office has 800 Negro employees, of whom 73 percent are nonprofessionals. While the number of Negroes in the upper ranks recently went from 24 to 80 in only three years, the disproportionate skew of the races is still clearly evident as one moves up from the floors on which routine operations are in motion to those where more professional tasks are carried out. The absence of Negro professionals reflects in large part the fact that Negroes have not been going into engineering, from which field the office draws much of its professional staff. At any time there tend to be vacancies in the professional positions, for the qualifications are relatively stringent.

The bad reputation of the Patent Office was in part derived from a rather poor promotion system, and some of the lack of communication in social courtesies also extended to official communications. Thus, vacancy notices were not posted openly; instead jobs were filled secretly, with evidence of favoritism.

{132} In addition, the Patent Office has had a completely archaic system for filing its printed patent information in cubicles in the basement, rather than a modern retrieval arrangement; the Office, for years, tried to sell the latter to Congress, but it has only very recently succeeded. The old system will therefore soon be abandoned. The bins in the basement were originally designed for male employees, but the classification rating and the pay are so low that virtually all of the employees have for years been Negro women. The basement is far less than ideal in its working conditions, with mice, rats, paper mites, and other inconveniences—including the necessity for climbing on a plain wooden bar to reach the proper bin location, which poses a constant hazard for nylons and skirts. The cry of racism is just one of the factors in this situation.

The Patent Office has discovered that it is difficult to keep a balance of Negro and white employees in the same office. Its experience has been that after the percentage of Negro employees goes over 50, white workers withdraw more and more from the employment by requesting a transfer or leaving the agency. This "tipping" phenomenon has also been noted in the field of housing. This agency, like many others, has had discussions about the desirability of attempting to create a balance artificially, since there are available techniques, including recruitment in the field for specific positions, which would allow it to maintain a viable balance.[12]

The Reluctant Dragon: Agriculture. Described by one observer as "the last bulwark of the Confederacy," the Department of Agriculture has been resistant to many of the developments in the field of equal opportunity. In

---

[12] At the time the interviews took place, spring of 1963, such action was strictly lunchtime conversation and had not reached the level of serious policy consideration.

The Problem in the Departments

March 1965 after waiting discreetly for the election period to be over, the U.S. Commission on Civil Rights issued a highly critical report of the department. It found that the department consistently followed policies of unequal treatment in its programs of aid and education, giving financial and research and technical assistance in a discriminatory fashion.

As applied to staff, the double standard has taken various forms. These have included failure to recruit, employ, or upgrade Negroes, or permit them to serve white farmers; isolation of Negroes in separate offices or at segregated meetings; and providing Negro staff members {133} with in-service training of shorter duration than and with inferior content to that given white staff members. "...In some programs, effective service to Negroes has been made dependent upon the number of Negroes employed, on the untenable theory that Negro farmers should be served only by Negro staff."[13]

These charges are not new. In 1963 Senator Javits of New York had offered an amendment to an appropriation bill for Agriculture which would have curtailed payments to any state that applied its program in a discriminatory fashion, and the Senator indicated it was well known that there was such discrimination.[14] *Jet* on October 24, 1963, asserted "the most discriminatory government department is Agriculture."[15]

Other data bear this out. Even in total employment, Negroes still constituted only 4.5 percent of all in the department in 1965, while less than 1 percent of all GS 12-18 ratings were held by Negroes. The rate of progress implied indicates that the department had made minimal changes rather than drastically revising its programs found to be discriminatory.

As elsewhere in the government, a disproportionate share of Agriculture's increased Negro employment was in newer programs, particularly in agencies dealing with burgeoning consumer services and food inspection.

The President's reaction to the Civil Rights Commission report was to transmit it to the Secretary of Agriculture with orders to report within thirty days on corrective measures. Secretary Freeman indicated that progress was being made in the department, but substantially accepted the criticism as valid and took steps to alleviate the situation.[16] The Federal Extension Service was ordered to integrate its employees by July 1. The Agricultural Stabilization and Conservation Service and the Federal Housing Administration were to secure representation of Negroes on advisory committees and to guarantee

---

[13] U.S. Commission on Civil Rights, *Equal Opportunity in Farm Programs*.

[14] *Congressional Record*, Eighty-Eighth Congress, Second Session, September 26, 1963, pp. 18256ff, and December 5, 1963, pp. 22403ff.

[15] *Jet*, October 24, 1963, p. 13.

[16] *New York Times*, June 28, 1965, p. 12.

their participation in department-held elections for such posts.[17]

The Elite Agencies: State, Justice, and Treasury. The Department of State in theory is most receptive to the incorporation of Negroes into its service. The concept of representativeness is said to underlie the requirement of geographical distribution in the Rogers Act, which is basic legislation on selection of employees for the Foreign Service. The department has had several conferences on equal employment opportunity, has considered and made changes in its testing system, and has inaugurated programs to prepare Negro students for foreign service. It has made great strides in bringing Negroes in at the upper levels, and in fact its percentage of Negroes at the very top rankings is among the highest in the government. To some extent these people are concentrated in departments and functions concerned with African affairs. Steady progress in other units, however, is confirmed in year-by-year tables.

The Department of Justice has lagged quite a bit behind in the field of employment. It started from a poor position. In 1947 the Justice Department was the largest agency practicing substantially complete exclusion of Negroes from its clerical positions.[18] At that time, Bradbury found, it had only two Negro attorneys and their secretaries in the department, one of them hired by Tom Clark from the Committee on Fair Employment Practice.[19] From a 3 percent component of Negroes in the department in 1961, the percentage had grown to 5.2 in 1965. Negroes have been particularly sensitive to the low rate of participation of Negroes in the FBI. This reaction has been strong enough to result in occasional statements and stories indicating some degree of representation in that agency.[20]

About two-thirds of the employees in the Treasury Department are in Internal Revenue, which is now reputed to have one of the more effective equal employment programs in the federal service. While Treasury has maintained an average record, it is an averaging of Internal Revenue's successes with other agencies' relatively poor showing. In June 1963 for example, Treasury had 117 Negroes at GS 12-18, 110 of them in Internal Revenue, (The latter had about 85 percent of all {135} such positions in the department at that time.[21]) In Internal Revenue the equal employment opportunity program has em-

---

[17] U.S. Commission on Civil Rights, *Law Enforcement* (Washington, D.C.: Government Printing Office, November 1965), p. 25, indicates that Negro efforts to vote in Department of Agriculture elections are resisted by tactics similar to those in regular elections.

[18] Bradbury, "Racial Discrimination in the Federal Service," pp. 101-102.

[19] A conversation in 1964 with Mr. Maceo Hubbard, then of the Department of Justice, indicated there was actually a third attorney in the department who was not generally identified as a Negro at the time of Bradbury's study.

[20] Bradbury, "Racial Discrimination in the Federal Service," pp. 102-104.

[21] Derived from "Number of Employees on the Rolls" (mimeographed internal report, Treasury Department, 1964).

ployed former personnel officers whose job is in part to maintain cordial relations with their former colleagues, while spending considerable time in recruitment.

The Post Office: Continuous Progress. In many ways the Post Office is the most decentralized operation of all with some 20,000 to 30,000 front-line executives. Each postmaster is virtually a law unto himself, and therefore what is suggested at the center of the structure is not always what is done at the periphery. In the face of this, the Post Office has made impressive progress. Assistant Postmaster General Richard Murphy has earned a considerable reputation for himself generally, and in the civil rights field particularly, as a "doer."

As mentioned in an earlier chapter the department has a unique corps of hearing officers who are ordinary post office employees trained to make investigations when complaints are filed. They hear cases only in installations other than their own and the department has, on the whole, moved to make its rulings stick. Furthermore its emphasis upon positive recruitment, its pattern of local committees, and its general inventiveness make the Post Office program an envied one.

In general, Negro groups are at maximum force in the Post Office. Historically, they were not permitted to join white postal unions and were separately organized. However, the Post Office was always considered a good employer by Negroes, and they moved into it in considerable numbers in the North. (Immediately after the merit system went into effect in 1883 a colored man took the examination for mail carrier and was appointed a substitute.) Even in the South, hiring of Negroes in the service has gone on and their civil service status has meant that Negro postmen have often been in the forefront of the civil rights movement in the South.[22]

Since they have accumulated seniority in the system, Negroes are presently available for supervisory positions. The basically undifferentiated structure of the service, requiring experience and judgment of the higher level bureaucrats but few skills, has also helped enable the Negro to move forward with great rapidity in this department, As one {136} expert in the area pointed out, the Post Office almost by definition will achieve a good record over the years in the promotion of Negroes, for accumulative service resulting from past practices will make itself felt in the future. This is not to say that the department has favored the Negro, or that there have not been numerous instances of discrimination, but rather that in many areas of the country the Post Office has seemed to Negroes an obvious and desirable place for employment.

In 1935 Harold Gosnell ventured a study of Negro politics in Chicago. He

---

[22] Leon Friedman, *Southern Justice* (New York: Pantheon, 1965), p. 170; Herman Miller, *Rich Man, Poor Man* (New York: Crowell, 1964), pp. 91-93, expressly mentions the Post Office.

found a topic of importance in the Chicago Post Office, devoting a full chapter and parts of others to employment in that particular segment of the federal service.[23] His figures were admittedly subject to error, yet his remains the most detailed study of any local situation. According to his figures, there was a rapid increase in Negro employment in the Chicago postal service:

Year	Number
1893	78
1900	135
1910	566
1921	1,400
1930	over 3,000

Negroes constituted about 14 percent of all employees of the Chicago Post Office in the 1920's and about 25 percent by 1930.[24] (Gosnell noted that the relatively desirable salary made the postal workers "among the best livers of Chicago's south side."[25]) In 1928 Congressman Stevenson of South Carolina read into the *Congressional Record* a criticism from a local Chicago group arguing that the Chicago Post Office employed too many Negroes, an early harbinger of the "reverse discrimination" charge.[26]

As of July 1966 Post Office officials, still operating under the headcount system, estimated that more than 65 percent of its 26,000 Chicago employees were Negro—that is to say, about 17,000 Negroes were so employed, They also estimated that new hiring was even more pronouncedly Negro, reaching perhaps 80 to 90 percent of all new employees. {137} Personnel officers believe a Negro majority came about shortly after World War II. In 1966 a Negro postmaster was appointed.

Social Security: Marking Time? Civil rights advocates believe that some of the problems with the Social Security Administration have come about as a consequence of its location in Baltimore, which has the character of a southern city. Certainly there are indications that the Social Security Administration has been inordinately unresponsive to advances made in the field of racial relations over the years. For example, figures are available from Social Security files on the racial classification of its employees in years in which it was believed that no governmental agency could legally compile such records.

---

[23] Harold Gosnell, *Negro Politicians in Chicago* (Chicago: University of Chicago Press, 1935), Chapter XIV.

[24] *Ibid.*, pp. 302-3.

[25] *Ibid.*, p. 305.

[26] *Congressional Record*, Seventieth Congress, First Session, February 2, 1928, pp. 2390-2392.

The Problem in the Departments

The racial problem is exaggerated and perhaps created by the nature of the agency, which requires large amounts of low-level work, involving little discretion and skill, and work of considerable professionalization and skill by an elite at the top. There is little opportunity for ladder-like promotion, and demands for promotions are difficult to satisfy within the existing structure. Efforts to upgrade the skills of the employees have had some effect, but there is little accommodation within the structure for this type of venture. In 1964 pressure on the Social Security Administration, both in Baltimore and in some of its field centers, resulted in special evaluative committees being appointed to deal with equal employment problems.[27] Even a reading of the official reports indicates that the agency has had serious problems in administrative technique, and has lagged behind comparable organizations in the handling of its racial problems. As elsewhere only a part of the difficulty is racial. Often bad management technique has in recent years been given attention only if tied to a complaint of racial discrimination. The resultant tightening of management has been one of the serendipitous benefits of the civil rights effort.

III

As early as 1955, Bradbury classified the federal agencies in terms of their attitudes (as of 1948) on nonwhite employment, and attempted to formulate propositions to account for the different patterns. Three major conclusions emerged: (1) Old-line agencies were more likely {138} to discriminate than newer ones. (2) Those with financial and business constituencies, including "liberal" regulatory agencies, were more likely to discriminate. Those with "welfare" and minority group constituencies were less likely to discriminate. (3) Mass organizations with routinized tasks were more likely to have large numbers of Negro employees and to maintain segregated units.[28]

Of these generalizations the first two remain as valid today as when they were put forward by Bradbury. In most instances, the organizations appear to maintain precisely the same rank order of acceptance or nonacceptance of Negroes as they did in 1948. It is in the area of the third proposition that considerable progress has been made, and certainly the advances that have occurred have statistically been principally in this type of structure.

Such organizations as the Veterans Administration, the General Services Administration, the Social Security Administration, the Post Office, and even the Patent Office have been obvious points for administrative pressure. Encouraged by external forces, Negro employees have learned to use their

---

[27] "Report of the Social Security Administration Advisory Committee on Personnel Practices in Baltimore" (mimeographed, 1964); "Report of the Advisory Work Group on Personnel Policies and Practices of the Philadelphia Program Center" (mimeographed, 1984).

[28] Bradbury, "Racial Discrimination in the Federal Service," pp. 106-107.

internal power as well. The Negro press has regularly—and not uniformly wisely or even fairly—made such organizations targets of publicity. Administrators faced with internal morale problems and external recruiting difficulties find it organizationally desirable to improve racial conditions. In short the agencies with the biggest problems in Washington are generally the easiest to begin to reform. In the equal employment program, thus, compliance is easiest where the situation is worst; this sets it off from such programs as school integration where progress must be from the border or fringe areas first. Of the two types of situations, the former lends itself more easily to solution. When the bulwarks are breached, the countryside is usually easily taken. In some instances, however, survival of the old discriminatory patterns in these mass organizations will persist at the upper reaches.

The over-all pattern of discrimination and compliance agency by agency persists. The forces at work—constituency pressure, differential prestige and the ability to withstand executive policies, and community pressures based upon the locale of operations—have proved to be perduring elements within which the program operates. This is revealed by rank order correlations and their remarkable stability from 1961 to {139} 1965 as well as by comparison with Bradbury's more impressionistic findings. See Tables 5 and 6.

Slight variations in this rank order indicate also some fluctuations of organizational ability to withstand administrative pressure as well as other mitigating factors. For example, the Navy has been most vigorous in its civilian program, possibly because its personnel policies are still considered rather questionable by Negro groups. Purely executive agencies have not proven to be more responsive than independent agencies, except where the more prestigious "commercial" constituencies of the latter groups have made them less responsive than the average. Congressional and executive "pets"—including such organizations as the Bureau of the Budget as an example of the latter, and the FBI as an example of the former—have complied with the program with less alacrity than others who see themselves as more completely dependent upon the President.

Those responsible for elements of the program are more likely to move vigorously, bearing in mind their "showcase" role as well as their functional responsibilities in this area. Thus the Civil Service Commission sharply stepped up its rate of employment of Negroes as it assumed responsibility for the program. The remarkable change in employment of Negroes in the office of the Secretary of Defense reflects this situation as well.

Expanding structures are of course more responsive to equal employment demands since they can be more easily accommodated within the goals of the organization, and in fact employment of members of groups regarded as "submarginal" but who can perform effectively is an efficient method of recruiting new personnel in a competitive labor market. Thus within the Department of Agriculture it has proven easier to hire Negroes for the new urban inspection services—poultry and the like—than to try to bring them into the older services.

The Problem in the Departments

It would appear that organizations that have recently experienced loss of prestige are also sensitive to administrative policies, and more likely to comply, but that organizations that have had a long-range tendency to decline in importance and prestige are more likely to persist in whatever policies have prevailed. That is to say, there appears to be a tendency for an organization with a short-range loss to attempt to restore its importance, but after a while it accepts this secular trend and goes along with it. {140 and 142: *tables*}

{142} Individual actions do have short-run effects, and of course, implementation is ultimately an individual function. Yet the regularities of chance seem to provide each structure with its share of divergent types. The efforts of individuals like Secretary of Agriculture Freeman also seem to have limited impact, without external machinery. For all of the occasional peaks and valleys, structured behavior seems the rule.

Table 5. Rank Order of Agencies in the Minority Group Census in 1961

Agency	Percentage of Negro Employment, Civil Service*	Rank	Percentage in GS 5-18	Rank
Department of State	7.6	18	4.4	10
Department of the Treasury	9.5	14	3.1	16
Department of Defense	7.5	20	4.2	12
Secretary of Defense	2.9	31	1.4	23
Department of the Army	9.1	15	5.0	6
Department of the Navy	7.6	18	4.0	13
Department of the Air Force	5.4	25	3.2	14
Department of Justice	5.0	29	1.3	21
Post Office Department	6.4	23	1.8	19
Department of the Interior	2.5	32	2.0	18
Department of Agriculture	3.0	31	1.5	22
Department of Commerce	9.9	13	4.6	9
Department of Labor	17.3	7	7.9	1
Department of Health, Education, and Welfare	15.0	9	7.5	2
Veterans Administration	21.2	4	7.0	3
Federal Aviation Agency	2.2	33	1.6	20
General Services Administration	17.3	7	4.8	8
National Aeronautics and Space Administration	1.7	34	1.6	20
Tennessee Valley Authority	†		†	
Housing and Home Finance Agency	9.1	15	4.3	11
Atomic Energy Commission	1.7	34	1.2	24
Government Printing Office	34.2	2	†	
Selective Service System	4.4	26	†	
Civil Service Commission	21.4	3	4.9	7
United States Information Agency	11.4	11	6.7	4
Small Business Administration	4.4	26	†	
Interstate Commerce Commission	12.3	10	†	
Railroad Retirement Board	19.4	6	†	
National Labor Relations Board	11.1	12	6.6	5
Smithsonian Institution	21.2	4	†	
Federal Communications Commission	6.2	24	3.2	14
Securities and Exchange Commission	7.9	17	2.8	17
Federal Deposit Insurance Corporation	3.3	28	†	
Federal Home Loan Bank Board	0.9	36	†	
Federal Trade Commission	6.7	22	†	
Federal Power Commission	6.9	21	†	
United States Soldiers' Home	51.3	1	†	

SOURCE: U.S. Civil Service Commission, *Study of Minority Group Employment in the Federal Government* (Washington, D.C.: Government Printing Office, 1963).
*Unlike Table 6, which gives 1965 data, this table includes only those under civil service, not all pay plans, and includes worldwide employment.
†Other pay plans.

The Problem in the Departments

Table 6. Rank Order of Agencies in the Minority Group Census in 1965

Agency	Percentage of Negro Employment, All Pay Plans*	Rank	Percentage in GS 5–18	Rank
Summary	9.5		5.3	
Department of State	10.8	22	18.4	1
Department of the Treasury	13.8	13	5.1	18
Department of Defense	11.6	20	5.0	19
Secretary of Defense	19.2	9	9.4	6
Department of the Army	11.8	19	5.6	17
Department of the Navy	13.8	13	4.8	20
Department of the Air Force	7.8	27	3.3	24
Department of Justice	5.2	31	2.5	25
Post Office Department	15.7	11	7.3	12
Department of the Interior	4.1	33	2.2	27
Department of Agriculture	4.5	32	2.5	25
Department of Commerce	13.4	16	6.7	14
Department of Labor	20.8	6	13.9	2
Department of Health, Education, and Welfare	19.9	8	10.0	4
Veterans Administration	24.7	5	8.9	7
Federal Aviation Agency	3.6	34	2.0	29
General Services Administration	34.0	4	8.1	9
National Aeronautics and Space Administration	3.2	35	1.9	30
Tennessee Valley Authority	7.0	28	*	
Housing and Home Finance Agency	13.0	17	7.3	12
Atomic Energy Commission	4.3	33	2.1	28
Government Printing Office	41.0	2	*	
Selective Service System	5.7	30	*	
Civil Service Commission	20.6	7	7.7	10
United States Information Agency	9.8	24	10.0	4
Small Business Administration	8.8	26	4.7	21
Interstate Commerce Commission	11.5	21	*	
Railroad Retirement Board	19.0	10	7.5	11
National Labor Relations Board	13.5	15	8.4	8
Smithsonian Institution	35.7	3	11.8	3
Federal Communications Commission	12.1	18	5.9	16
Securities and Exchange Commission	10.6	23	4.7	21
Federal Deposit Insurance Corporation	6.1	29	*	
Federal Home Loan Bank Board	3.2	35	*	
Federal Trade Commission	9.2	25	3.6	23
Federal Power Commission	14.9	12	6.7	14
United States Soldiers' Home	46.8	1	*	

SOURCE: U.S. Civil Service Commission, *Study of Minority Group Employment in the Federal Government* (Washington, D.C.: Government Printing Office, 1965).
*Other pay plans.

Conclusions

{143}
STUDIES of political socialization have in the past concentrated mostly upon the childhood educational experience of individuals. It remained for T. H. Marshall to point out that unionism was a form of secondary or industrial-relations "citizenship" which in effect supplemented traditional political participation and on the whole was separated off from childhood experiences. In addition, he has pointed out that education has similarly operated not only as the scene of childhood training but also as a secondary structure involving its own type of participation.[1] Thus socialization emerges as a continuous lifetime process.

Certainly the prospect for implementation of new concepts of citizenship, and new approaches to political participation, would be most discouraging if indeed it were true that change could be induced only from the time of birth through the first few years. There is, however, no strong reason to believe that such is the case. Herbert Hyman has compiled numerous studies which suggest the basic importance of the early years. But these and other studies also show that differentiation and proliferation of attitudes persist through later years.[2] Probably the {144} general preoccupation with the first few years of life is a consequence of the fact that those who first introduced political socialization as a popular study were psychologists.

Perhaps it is only realistic to assume that groups of individuals will persist in their traditional political orientation, but this is also the easy and standard assumption, as often based upon ignorance as upon fact: "That which has been must be." Enough evidence of successes in induction of change in societies abounds to encourage further social engineering. Then, too, there is evidence that it is difficult to induce change in the young without accompanying behavioral variation on the part of the older generation.[3]

The federal equal employment program—whether consciously so or not—suggests that the governmental sector is not merely the instrument for induction of change, "the vanguard of equality," but the means of change itself. Bayard Rustin, the unofficial philosopher of the civil rights movement, has pointed out that in the past Negro progress has occurred largely as a conse-

---

[1] T. H. Marshall, *Class, Citizenship and Social Development* (New York: Doubleday, 1964), especially pp. 94 and 109-110.

[2] Herbert Hyman, *Political Socialization* (Glencoe, Ill.: Free Press, 1959), especially pp. 25-68.

[3] Sidney Verba, *Small Groups and Political Behavior* (Princeton, N.J.: Princeton University Press, 1961), p. 55.

quence of the expansion of the public sector.[4] Radicals among the civil rights workers have extrapolated the conclusion that a radical reorganization of society with some sort of socialistic expansion of the public sector is the major hope for the Negro community. (But perhaps it would be more accurate to say that their hopes for a socialistic reorganization of the public sector seem at present to be achievable only through the civil rights movement. That is to say, they have identified the Negro as the substitute for a proletariat that somehow has not harkened to their appeals.) But a more modest and quite conservative view also recognizes that the public sector is at once the showcase of society, the harbinger of change for the private sector, and a training ground for the induction of change.

George Washington Cable, with his usual perspicacity, pointed out at the turn of the century the tragic position of the Negro in the public life of his country. He suggested that having failed to secure proportional representation in the public sector, the Negro would have to settle for the claim of merit, a claim which other groups rely upon only infrequently.[5] But on gaining a measure of political strength and self-confidence the Negro community has turned, at least to some extent, from emphasis on merit to renewed claims for proportionate representation, Most ethnic groups have, after all, taken the stance that genetic ability is more or less uniformly distributed throughout the population and that the absence of proportional representation in the carrying out of the various functions in the community is an indication of discrimination. The Negro came late to this position but he now espouses it vigorously. And he regards proportional representation in the public service as the sine qua non. For if the government will not accord him his just place, the private sector will clearly not do so.

There are certain elements at variance with reality in the stance of the Negro community, for it is clear that in terms of training and past experience the Negro is at a disadvantage vis-à-vis his white competitors, regardless of his innate potentialities. In both the public and the private sector the temporary solution to the problem of differential employment lies in a shrewd assessment of where increased Negro employment will not prove deleterious to society, given the somewhat lesser than average developed talents available in the Negro community.

Even in the short run, however, it would appear that the burden of proof lies with those who wish to maintain anything approaching the status quo. In worldwide perspective it would appear that the discrepancy in background between the Negro and white communities in the United States is less than the difference in reward and position between the two. It is, for example, striking that if one applies the index suggested by Harbison and Myers as a

---

[4] Bayard Rustin, "From Protest to Politics," *Commentary*, February 1965, p. 28.

[5] George Washington Cable, *The Negro Question* (New York: Scribner's, 1890), pp. 79-80.

Conclusions

measure of the differences between societies in development of human resources, the American Negro community emerges with extremely high ratings.[6] This measure—based upon the percentage of young people in secondary schools and colleges, with heavier weighting to the college component differentiates clearly between underdeveloped, partially developed, semi-advanced, and advanced nations. Indexes were developed from 1962 and 1964 data on American Negroes in secondary schools and colleges. As shown in Table 7, American Negroes in 1962 would have ranked at about the level the Soviet Union had reached at the time Harbison and Myers compiled their index (1958-1959). The index for two years later {146: *table 7*} {147} shows an amazing increase of 12 points, moving the Negro community above the level of Canada.

To be sure these comparisons cannot be regarded as rigorous. It can be assumed that, with all the recent emphasis upon social development in the world, many if not most countries especially the advanced ones—would have had higher index scores in 1962 and 1964 than in 1958-1959. Furthermore, Harbison and Myers warn that their data are the best available but not highly reliable in many instances. Then, too, the crudity of the index was as well recognized by the originators as it will be by any reader. Even in the original study, the authors warned against attaching importance to a specific placement on the table for any country, and this warning would apply, in compounded form, for the more artificial use made of the index here. Finally, this simple weighting scheme was not, of course, intended to be applied to parts of nations. But even the rough comparison we have been able to make is suggestive: although the difference we find between the white and Negro communities in the United States is striking, there would seem to be more in common between the Negro and white in level of background than between the United States as a whole and many countries whose technological skill we admire and on occasion envy.

Traditionally, as noted in earlier chapters, government service has been recognized by the American Negro community as an attractive source of jobs, a view based upon economic realities. Kilpatrick and his associates found that Negroes had a more positive view of governmental employment than whites, even with adjustment for type of position and status in the bureaucracy.[7] But

---

[6] Frederick Harbison and Charles Myers, *Education, Manpower and Economic Growth* (New York: McGraw-Hill, 1984), p. 33.

[7] Franklin P. Kilpatrick, Milton Cummings, Jr., and M. Kent Jennings, *The Image of the Federal Service* (Washington D.C.: Brookings, 1964), pp. 96, 159, 225.

Table 7. Countries Grouped by Level of Human Resources Development in 1958–1959, as Measured by a Composite Index, with "Placement" of the American Negro Community on the Basis of 1962 and 1964 Data Indicated

Country	Index	Country	Index
Level I, Underdeveloped		*Level III, Semiadvanced*	
Niger	0.3	Mexico	33.0
Ethiopia	0.75	Thailand	35.1
Nyasaland	1.2	India	35.2
Somalia	1.55	Cuba	35.5
Afghanistan	1.9	Spain	39.6
Saudi Arabia	1.9	South Africa	40.0
Tanganyika	2.2	Egypt	40.1
Ivory Coast	2.6	Portugal	40.8
Northern Rhodesia	2.95	Costa Rica	47.3
Congo	3.55	Venezuela	47.7
Liberia	4.1	Greece	48.5
Kenya	4.75	Chile	51.2
Nigeria	4.95	Hungary	53.9
Haiti	5.3	Taiwan	53.9
Senegal	5.45	South Korea	55.0
Uganda	5.45	Italy	56.8
Sudan	7.55	Yugoslavia	60.3
		Poland	66.5
Level II, Partially Developed		Czechoslovakia	68.9
Guatemala	10.7	Uruguay	69.8
Indonesia	10.7	Norway	73.8
Libya	10.85		
Burma	14.2	*Level IV, Advanced*	
Dominican Republic	14.5	Denmark	77.1
Bolivia	14.8	Sweden	79.2
Tunisia	15.25	Argentina	82.0
Iran	17.3	Israel	84.9
China (Mainland)	19.5	West Germany	85.8
Brazil	20.9	Finland	88.7
Colombia	22.6	American Negro (1962)	91.8
Paraguay	22.7	U.S.S.R.	92.9
Ghana	23.15	Canada	101.6
Malaya	23.65	American Negro (1964)	103.8
Lebanon	24.3	France	107.8
Ecuador	24.4	Japan	111.4
Pakistan	25.2	United Kingdom	121.6
Jamaica	26.8	Belgium	123.6
Turkey	27.2	Netherlands	133.7
Peru	30.2	Australia	137.7
Iraq	31.2	New Zealand	147.3
		United States	261.3

SOURCES: Frederick Harbison and Charles Myers, *Education, Manpower and Economic Growth* (New York: McGraw-Hill, 1964), p. 33. *Current Population Reports,* September 24, 1963 (Series P-20, no. 126), and *Statistical Abstract of the United States,* 1965, Table 142.

as studies by Cantril and Kilpatrick have shown, Negro expectations of social improvement are very high.[8] Aware of their current low status and of their slow progress in the past, Negroes have expectations of future advances that exceed even those of junior executives, a highly ambitious and mobile group.

Not only is the level of expectation high, but the sensitivity of Negroes to small differences and small slights remains at a high level, while {148} achievement is judged in terms of progress in both tiny symbolic matters and major accomplishments. Thus President Kennedy was viewed with favor not only because of his intensive general program, but also because of the attention he paid to small matters. It was remembered by Negro leaders years afterwards that the President had called the Coast Guard to account for the absence of any Negro faces in the contingent that marched in his inaugural parade.[9] Such attention to details is hard to sustain on a day-to-day basis, and yet it must be achieved.

With each year the impact of the equal employment program in the federal service continues to grow. This is measurable not only in numbers but also in level of participation of Negro officeholders and the degree to which important policy matters of a general nature, not strictly ethnic in content, have been entrusted to Negroes.

It has been almost as easy to move a high percentage (but small numbers) of Negroes into very high positions as to place large numbers of Negroes into lower-grade positions. The level of education of the Negro community is impressive in the light of historic achievements of other communities throughout the world. As Herbert Hill has pointed out, the number of Negro Ph.D.'s in the United States exceeds the number of Negro plumbers[10]—and while this is in part a tribute to the effectiveness of the exclusionary policies of the plumbers, it also indicates the extent to which Negroes have embraced higher education. It has thus been relatively easy—although not the easiest task—to find Negro bureau chiefs and a Cabinet secretary, some assistant secretaries, and administrative assistants to departmental secretaries. What is more significant are the signs that the equal employment opportunity program is succeeding in bringing in middle-level bureaucrats who in time will take their places at the higher civil service positions. The ultimate success of the program will not be measured in the number of generals and colonels, but in the accumulation of people at the "staff sergeant" functional level, who are

---

[8] They asked individuals throughout the world to indicate where they stood in the social scale and where they expected to stand ten years hence. They provided a ladder diagram which allowed the respondent to place himself without regard to any particular verbal designation. Thus cultural factors were kept at a minimum, Franklin Kilpatrick and Hadley Cantril, "Self-Anchored Scale: A Measure of Individuals' Unique Reality World," *Journal of Individual Psychology*, 16: 7 (1960).

[9] *Crisis*, June-July 1963, p. 343.

[10] Public lecture, Michigan State University, spring 1963.

the sinews of the career service. At this writing progress is being made in precisely this fashion.

Perhaps the finest tribute to the equal employment opportunity program is the extent to which it is being imitated. The emulation of the slogans of equality in other organizations, indeed the adopting of the {149} program name itself, is one such index, although a minor one. The emulation in terms of program is perhaps more impressive. Efforts within the bureaucracy to lessen discrimination against other groups—other minorities like women and the handicapped have drawn upon the experience and success of the equal employment program. The President's Commission on the Status of Women has been engaged in ventures similar to those of the President's committee and it has compiled a number of reports suggesting the degree and nature of the problem of equal employment opportunity for women, Reflecting perhaps the greater complexity of the problem in this area and the absence of some of the overt political pressures involved, the reports and studies undertaken with regard to discrimination on the basis of sex in the federal service are to date franker and more subtle than those dealing with race.[11]

The equal employment program has also had desirable side effects, not connected with race. Many issues of bad management and indifference to the behavior of individual workers have come to the fore and have been discussed as a consequence of the equal employment program. That is to say, the issue of race can often be the basis for bringing to consciousness a problem that otherwise would have been treated with relative indifference.

It is, however, in its success in changing the status of the Negro and in signaling that change in the psyche of the Negro himself that the program will be judged. Considerable ingenuity has so far been employed in dealing with the most obvious manifestations of prejudice. In the future progress will require not merely improvement in administrative machinery and continued overt recruitment, but new forms of social engineering in areas where active hostility to Negro participation is most evident, and where sources of manpower are in the greatest supply. At least as much ingenuity will be needed in the future as in the past. Providing equality of opportunity which at first sight looks like a problem that can be solved simply by the stroking of a pen is in truth as complex as the total race problem itself.

Whatever the motivations behind the 1965 reorganization of the governmental machinery for dealing with equal employment opportunity, {150} it would probably have needed an overhaul in any event as a new stage in the life cycle of the racial problem had been reached. In this respect the Civil Service Commission has a challenging opportunity—an opportunity it seemingly seeks—to alter its historical image as an agency at most indifferent to the Negro community.

---

[11] See, for example, President's Commission on the Status of Women, *Report of the Committee on Federal Employment* (Washington, D.C.: Government Printing Office, 1968).

Conclusions

To this date, all the major social groupings of our society—business, labor, agriculture, immigrant groups—have achieved social and political standing through governmental aid and intervention.[12] The Negro community appears to be no exception to that historical tendency. What is unique is the extent to which the government is involved in Negro self-development and to which the bureaucracy is itself the arena for a struggle to achieve equal treatment of equal merit.

Other societies have faced similar multi-ethnic problems. Some have succeeded in dealing with them and some have not. It is clear—as stated at the outset of this study—that one of the ways in which our society will be judged throughout the world is in terms of our success in dealing with our racial problem generally, and if we cannot resolve it on the governmental level, we shall not resolve it at all.

---

[12] Kenneth Boulding, *The Organizational Revolution* (New York; Harper, 1953), pp. 51-52, 107, 111, 137-138. Boulding's main point is that the supply of organizational skill is the factor that has altered relations, rather than pent-up social needs.

Index

Page numbers below reference the original pagination, embedded into the text of this modern edition by the use of brackets.

Agriculture, Department of, 125, 127, 132-133, 139, 140, 141, 142

Air Force, 87, 116, 128, 129-130, 140, 141

Alabama, 104

Alexander, Will; and Negro spokesman in federal administration, 23-25; quoted on segregation in Washington, 28

American Soldier, The, 87

Antoine, C. C., 15

Aristotle, 82

Army, 128, 140, 141

Arthur, Chester A., 16

Aswell, James B., quoted, 20-21

Athens, 48

Baltimore, 137

Bassett, Ebenezer, 12

Belgium, 60, 61, 146

Bentley, A. F., 107

Berle, Adolph A., 73

Bethune, Mary McLeod, 24

Birth of a Nation, 20

"Black Cabinet" advisers, 23-25

Blau, Peter, 72

Blease, Coleman L., 22

Bowles, Chester, 92

Bradbury, William, 134, 139; analysis of World War II federal employment of Negroes, 32-33, 92-93; propositions on patterns of discrimination, 137-138

Bruce, B. K., 15, 16

Buchwald, Art, 100

Budget, Bureau of the, 127, 139

Bunche, Ralph, quoted, 25

Bureaucracy: emergence of, 49-50; Weber as analyst, 49-50, 52, 53; standards of loyalty, 50-51; Saint-Simon and concept of, 52

Burleson, Albert S., 20

Burnham, James, 53

Butler, Andrew, quoted, 10

Cable, George Washington, 144

Campbell, T. M., 25n

Canada, 60, 61, 146, 147

Cantril, Hadley, 147

Carpenter, Walter Seal, 55, 82n

Carter, Robert, quoted, 76n, 82

Catholics, lack of intellectual tradition among American, 62

Celebrezze, Anthony, 88, 114

Census Bureau, 18, 22

Chapman, Brian, quoted, 59, 60

Chicago, 15, 97, 136

China, 50, 146

Civil Rights, U.S. Commission on, 132, 133

Civil Rights Act of 1964, 40, 41, 42, 125

Civil Service Commission: regains fair employment functions, 6, 43, 45, 107-108, 114, 121-122; on number of Negro employees in *1892*, 19; and photograph policy, 21, 31; World War II role, 33-34; Fair Employment Board part of, 35; internal fair employment program, 101, 114-115, 127, 139, 140, 141; and complaints, 111; regional survey, 115-117; new rules and procedures, 117-118

131

Civil service reform: motives for, 54-55; and change in educational system, 52, 62
Civilian Conservation Corps (CCC), 23
Clark, Tom, 134
Classification system, for federal service, 19, 98, 100
Cleveland, Grover, 14, 16
Coast Guard, 148
Coleman, William, quoted, 55
Collins, Leroy, 104
Colorado, 95
Commerce, Department of, 22, 23-24, 26, 34, 44, 109, 140, 141
Community Relations Service, 41, 44, 104, 127
"Compensationist" argument for Negro employment, 76-85
Complaints on discrimination: World War II statistics, 34; President's committee record on, 39-40; procedures for, 117-119; differing standards on state and local levels, 119-121; utility as promoters of equal employment, 119
Connecticut, 11
"Corrective action," definition of, 40
Dallas, 77n, 95
Davis, John A.: quoted on wartime committee, 33-34; quoted on need for separate fair employment agency, 107
Defense, Department of, 112, 125, 127-130, 139, 140, 141
Democratic National Committee, 37, 41, 114-115
Democratic party: indifference to Negro in Reconstruction, 15-16; continued aloofness in *1932*, 22; New Deal generates new attitudes, 25-26
Denmark, 59, 146
DePriest, Oscar, 25-26
Dickens, Charles, 54
Dirksen, Everett, 42
District of Columbia, 11, 13, 14, 19, 103-105, 125
Douglass, Frederick, 12-14
DuBois, Frederick, on need to change Negro values, 102
Duncan, Otis Dudley, quoted, 103
Dungan, Ralph, 37
Dunmore, Lord, 8
Ebony, 130
"Echelon" merit, 70n, 82
Eisenhower, Dwight D., 35, 38-39, 107-108, 113
Elkins, Stanley, 7
Elliott, Robert, 15
Embree, Edwin K., 23-24
Equal employment officer (fair employment officer): established, 35; described, 38-39, 109, 111-113; evaluated in regional study, 116-118
Equal Employment Opportunity Commission: relation to President's committee, 40, 42, 43; policies, 69n, 80
Ervin, Sam, 111
Executive Order *8802*, 30, 31
Executive Order *10925*, 36, 42, 108, 109, 113
Executive Order *11197*, 42
Fair Employment Board, 35
Fair Employment Practice, Committee on, 30-35, 99, 107, 134
Fair employment practices commissions (state), 35-36
Fay, Horace, Jr., 181
FBI, 134, 139
Feild, John, 36-37, 121
Fischer, John, 55
Fleming, Harold, 121
Foner, Phillip, 13
Ford, Henry, 73
Foreign Service, 84, 113, 134
Foreman, Clark, 24
Fox, Richard T., 109
France, 52, 59, 80, 146
Franklin, John Hope, quoted, 25
Freedman's Bank, 13

Index

Freedman's Bureau, 12, 22
Freeman, Orville L., 133, 142
Garfield, James, 14, 15, 54n
Garfinkel, Herbert, 29
Gavagan, Joseph, 26
General Services Administration, 138, 140, 141
Georgia, 15
Germany, 53, 146
Glatt, Carl, 119-120
Goffman, Erving, 70n
Goldwater, Barry, 40
Gosnell, Harold, 136
Granger, Gideon, quoted, 9
Grant, Ulysses, 12, 13
Great Britain (United Kingdom), 54, 56, 57, 62, 91, 146
Haiti, 12, 14, 20, 146
Hamilton, Alexander, 55
Hampton, Wade, 17
Harbison, Frederick, 145-147
Harding, Warren G., 22
Harrison, Benjamin, 14
Hastie, William, 24, 25n
Hayes, Laurence J. W., 19-20
Hayes, Rutherford B., 13, 15, 16
Health, Education, and Welfare, Department of, 38, 125, 140, 141
Heflin, J. Thomas, 22
Hill, Herbert, 111, 120, 148
Hitler, Adolf, 52
Hobbes, Thomas, 82
Hofstadter, Richard, 124
Holland (Netherlands), 59, 60, 146
Hooker, Richard, 82
Hoover, Herbert, 22
Hope, John, II, 36
Horton, Ralph, 128
Howard University, 27, 113
Humphrey, Hubert, 41-44
Hunt, H. D., 25n
Hyman, Herbert, 143

Ickes, Harold, 23-24
Illinois, 8, 11, 26, 42
India, 3, 61-62, 146
Indiana, 8, 16
Interior, Department of the, 22, 23, 24, 140, 141
Internal Revenue Service, 112, 134-135
Israel, 60, 62, 63, 77, 103, 146
Jackson, Andrew, 8, 55, 56
Jacksonian "spoils" concept, 47, 55-56
Javits, Jacob, 133
Jefferson, Thomas, quoted, 55
Jet, 133
Jews, contrasted with Negroes, 63
Johnson, Andrew, 12, 13
Johnson, Charles, 24
Johnson, Lyndon B., 36, 38, 40, 41, 105, 108, 133
Jones, Eugene Kinckle, 25n
Justice, Department of, 18, 41, 44, 101, 116, 127, 134, 140, 141
Kalven, Harry, Jr., quoted, 4
Kansas, 119, 120
Katzenbach, Nicholas, 44n
Kennedy, John F., 36, 39, 108, 113, 148
Kennedy, Robert F., 37
Kilpatrick, F. P., 147
King, Martin Luther, 125n
Kingsley, J. Donald, and concept of representative bureaucracy, 48, 54-55, 57, 59
Kristol, Irving, 100
Ku Klux Klan, 16
Labor, Department of, 24, 37, 41, 45, 108, 109, 111, 140, 141
La Guardia, Fiorello, 30
Lamar, L. Q. C., 15, 16
Leacock, Stephen, quoted, 5
Lebanon, 61
Lenin, V. I., 52
Leskes, Theodore, 35
Lewis, William H., 18
Liberia, 14, 146

Lichtman, Richard, quoted, 79-80
Litwack, Leon, quoted, 10
Locke, John, 82
London, 50
Longworth, Nicholas, 26
Louisiana, 15, 20
Lowe, Robert, quoted, 55
Lyell, Sir Charles, 10
Lynch, John, 15, 18
McAdoo, William, 20
McCamy, James, 57
McKinley, William, 16
McLean, John, 10
McNamara, Robert, 129
Macy, John, 38, 108, 110, 114
Maine, 10
Malayan Federation, 62
Mann, Theophilius, 25n
March on Washington of *1941*, 29-30
Marshall, T. H., 143
Marshall, Thurgood, 41
Marsilius of Padua, 48
Martin, Louis, 37, 114
Massachusetts, 17
Meany, George, 45
Michels, Robert, 52
Michigan, 95
Miller, Herman, 89, 93, 104
Miller, Kelly, 20n, 21.
Minneapolis, 115-116, 119
Minnesota, 41, 121
Minority census of employment, 38, 104-105, 110, 140, 141
Mississippi, 14, 15, 16, 104, 106
Mitchell, Arthur W., 21n
Morgan, Richard, 43, 44, 45
Mosca, Gaetano, 52
Moses, Earl R., 25n
Moyers, Bill, 44n
Murphy, Richard, 135
Myers, Charles, 145-147
Myrdal, Gunnar, 4

National Aeronautics and Space Administration, 110, 140, 141
National Association for Inter-Group Relations, 113
National Association for the Advancement of Colored People, 23, 111
NRA, deleterious effects on Negro employment, 27
Navy, 21, 109, 128, 129, 139, 140, 141
Nebraska, 11
Negro and the First Amendment, The, 4
Negro employment in federal service: at time of Pendleton Act, 19; in Wilson administration, 19-20; post-World War I, 22; in New Deal period, 22-23; during World War II, 32-33; changing distribution by grades, *1961-1967,* 100-101; in Washington, 104; in regions, 104-105
Negro suffrage: pre-Civil War, 8, 10-11; post-Civil War, 11; turn of century, 18-19
New Deal, and Negro progress, 22-27
New Jersey, 10, 35
New Leader, 44, 45
New York City, 11, 60
New York State, 8, 11, 35, 133
New York World's Fair, 69n
Nixon, Richard, 35
Nkrumah, Kwame, 124n
North Carolina, 15, 17, 26, 95
Northcote-Trevelyan report, 54
Office of Education, 34
Office of Production Management (OPA), 34, 92
Officeholding, as symbol of political power, 5, 11-12, 47, 91
Ohio, 8, 11
Oklahoma, 86
Oregon, 8
Oxley, Lawrence A., 25n
Pareto, Vilfredo, 52
Parsons, Talcott, 72
Patent Office, 131-132, 138

Index

Patterson, A. E., 20
Paid, Norman, 128
Pendleton Act, 19, 56, 106
Pennsylvania, 11, 96
Phillips, Seth, 119, 120
Pierce, J. B., 25n
Plato, 65
Post Office, 9-10, 20, 22, 34, 98, 101, 109, 110, 111, 112, 117, 120, 125, 135-137, 138, 140, 141: Washington, 26; Dallas, 77n; Minneapolis, 115-116; Chicago, 136-137
Prebendary system, 49
President's Commission on Human Rights, 33
President's Commission on the Status of Women, 149
President's Committee on Equal Employment Opportunity, 6; as established and Johnson named chairman of, 36; internal operations, 37-39; accomplishments, 39-40; Humphrey named chairman of, 41; difficulties with Congress and abolition, 42-45; procedures established by, 108-111
President's Committee on Government Contract Compliance, 35
President's Committee on Government Contracts, 35, 36, 39
President's Committee on Government Employment Policy, 35, 39
President's Council on Equal Opportunity, 42-44, 108
Public service, as source of employment, 5, 90-91, 93-94, 96-97
Pyle, Christopher, 43, 44, 45
Quotas: religious, caste, or ethnic, 61-62; geographic, 61; "benign," 78-77, 82
Ramspeck, Robert, 32
Randolph, A. Philip, 29
Reconstruction, 11-16 *passim*
Religion, as obstacle to representative bureaucracy, 60-61
Republican party, attitude toward Negro public service, 13-14, 18-19

Revolutionary War, 8
Rhode Island, 11
Richardson, J. P., quoted, 17
Riesman, David, 99
Robertson, A. Willis, 42-43
Rogers Act, 134
Roosevelt, Eleanor, 30
Roosevelt, Franklin D., 22, 24, 29, 30, 35, 38, 107
Roosevelt, Theodore, 17, 18
Rosenwald Fund, 22, 24
Rostow, W. W., 28
Royal Commission on Bi-Lingualism and Bi-Culturalism (Canada), quoted, 60
Royal Commission on the Civil Service (Great Britain), quoted, 56
Ruling Servants, The, 46
Russell Amendment, 34-35
Rustin, Bayard, 144
Saint-Simon, Comte de, 52
San Francisco, 95
Santo Domingo, 13, 14
Schurz, Carl, 13
Segregation: in Census Bureau, 18; in Wilson administration, 20-22; elimination in agencies, 22, 23; in congressional lunchroom, 26-27
Sephardim, 60, 62, 77
Sex, discrimination on basis of, 69, 149
Shakespeare, William, 65
Silberman, Charles, 77
Slade, William, 12
Social class, as obstacle to representative bureaucracy, 59, 61
Social Security Administration, 38, 97, 113, 114, 137, 138
South Africa, 87, 146
South Carolina, 15, 17, 136
South Tyrol, 59
Spika, Eugene, 115
Stampp, Kenneth, 17
Stanton, Edwin, 12

State, Department of, 101, 109, 113, 127, 134, 140, 141
State and local officeholding by Negroes: before Civil War, 10; Reconstruction period, 14-17; in recent years, 94-96
Stevenson, William F., 136
Stouffer, Samuel, 87
Strauss, Eric, 46
Sweden, 59, 146
Switzerland, 59
Taft, William Howard, 17-18
Taylor, Hobard, Jr., 40, 41, 44n
Tocqueville, Alexis De, quoted, 8
Treason of Clerks, The, 53
Treasury, Department of the, 20, 22, 125, 127, 134-135, 140, 141
Troutman, Robert, 36-37
Truman, Harry, 35, 107
Turner, Ralph, 53
Twain, Mark, 14
United Nations Charter, 61
USSR, 91, 145, 146
"Untouchables," 3, 61
Van Buren, Martin, 8
Vann, Robert L., 25n
Van Riper, Paul, 20, 21
Veterans Administration, 101, 109, 112, 116, 118, 119, 120, 125-126, 130-131, 138, 140, 141
Veterans preference, 69, 82n
Vice President, role in equal employment, 35, 36, 40, 41-45
War Manpower Commission, 34
Washington, Booker T., 18, 88
Washington, George, 8
Washington, D.C., 9, 19, 23-24, 26, 29, 32, 33, 93, 97, 103-105, 125
Weaver, Robert, 24
Weber, Max, 49-53, 56
Wechsler, Herbert, quoted, 81-82
Welles, Gideon, 12
West Indies, 4
Wharton, V. L., 16
White, George H., 15, 17
White, Lee, 37-38, 115
Wilkins, Roy, 44
William of Occam, 48
Williams, G. Mennen, 109
Wilson, James Q., 124
Wilson, Woodrow W., 14, 18, 19-21, 22
Wirtz, W. Willard, 44n, 45, 91, 110, 111
Wittfogel, Karl A., 50
Wofford, Harris, Jr., 37
Women: acceptance in civil service, 56-57; special employment situation of Negro, 97-98; President's Commission on the Status of, 149
Woodward, C. Vann, quoted, 13-14
World War I, 21, 33
World War II, 28, 66, 87, 89, 92, 123
Young, Whitney, Jr., quoted, 75n, 119

ABOUT THE AUTHOR

Samuel Krislov is Professor Emeritus of Political Science and Law at the University of Minnesota. The author or coauthor of some dozen books, including *Representative Bureaucracy, Compliance and the Law, The Supreme Court in the Political Process,* and *How Nations Choose Product Standards,* he is also a frequent contributor to political science and law reviews including the *Harvard Law Review, Supreme Court Law Review, Yale Law Journal, Publius, and Jurimetrics.*

He has taught as Visiting Professor at American University and the University of California, Berkeley Law School, as well as Fudan University in Shanghai, Tel Aviv University, and universities in Korea, Turkey, and Poland. He shared a position as a Distinguished Fulbright Professor at the Budapest Institute of Economic Sciences.

Krislov has served as President of the Midwest Political Science Association and the Law and Society Association, and as Chair of the National Research Council's Committee on Research on Law Enforcement and Justice. He has been a recipient of numerous grants and awards including Guggenheim, Bush, Ford Foundation, and Russell Sage fellowships. He has also received a residency at the Rockefeller Foundation at Bellagio and National Science Foundation grants. He was honored with a Lifetime Achievement Award from the Law and Courts Section of the American Political Science Association.

Visit us at *www.quidprobooks.com.*

www.ingramcontent.com/pod-product-compliance
Lightning Source LLC
Chambersburg PA
CBHW052101230426
43662CB00036B/1725